GCSE English Literature AQA Anthology

Relationships

The Study Guide Foundation Level

This book is a step-by-step guide to becoming an expert on the Anthology part of your GCSE English Literature exam.

It's got everything you need to know — annotated poems, key themes, exam advice and worked essays.

It's ideal for use as a classroom study book or a revision guide.

What CGP is all about

Our sole aim here at CGP is to produce the highest quality books — carefully written, immaculately presented and dangerously close to being funny.

Then we work our socks off to get them out to you — at the cheapest possible prices.

Contents

How to Use this Book 1

Section One — Poems from the Literary Heritage

Sonnet 116 — William Shakespeare 4
To His Coy Mistress — Andrew Marvell 6
The Farmer's Bride — Charlotte Mew 8
Sonnet 43 — Elizabeth Barrett Browning 10
Sister Maude — Christina Rossetti 12
Nettles — Vernon Scannell 14
Born Yesterday — Philip Larkin 16

Section Two — Contemporary Poems

The Manhunt — Simon Armitage 18
Hour — Carol Ann Duffy 20
In Paris With You — James Fenton 22
Quickdraw — Carol Ann Duffy 24
Ghazal — Mimi Khalvati 26
Brothers — Andrew Forster 28
Praise Song For My Mother — Grace Nichols 30
Harmonium — Simon Armitage 32

Section Three — Themes

Relationships 34
Negative Emotions 36
Love 37
Time 38
Getting Older 39
Death 40
Memory 41
Nature 42
Pain and Desire 43

Section Four — Poetry Techniques

Forms of Poetry 44
Poetic Devices 45
Beginnings of Poems 46
Couplets and Last Lines 47
Rhyme and Rhythm 48
Use of First Person 49
Imagery 50
Unusual Vocabulary 51
Irony and Sarcasm 52
Mood 53

Section Five — The Poetry Exam

The Poetry Exam: Unit Two Overview 54
Sample Question 1 55
Planning 56
How to Answer the Question 57
Mark Scheme 58
Sample Question 2 59
How to Answer the Question 60
Sample Question 3 62
How to Answer the Question 63

Section Six — Controlled Assessment

The Controlled Assessment 64

Section Seven — Writing Skills

Making Comparisons 68
Linking Words 69
Quoting 70
Structure 71

Glossary 72
Index 74
Acknowledgements 76

Published by CGP

Editors:
Heather Gregson, Luke von Kotze, Edward Robinson, Hayley Thompson, Karen Wells

Produced with:
Alison Smith, Peter Thomas, Nicola Woodfin

Contributors:
Caroline Bagshaw

With thanks to Rachael Powers and Emma Willshaw for the proofreading
and Jan Greenway for the copyright research.

ISBN: 978 1 84762 531 1

Groovy website: www.cgpbooks.co.uk
Jolly bits of clipart from CorelDRAW®
Printed by Elanders Ltd, Newcastle upon Tyne.

Based on the classic CGP style created by Richard Parsons.

Photocopying — it's dull, it takes ages… and sometimes it's a bit naughty. Luckily, it's dead cheap, easy and quick to order more copies of this book from CGP — just call us on 0870 750 1242. Phew!

Text, design, layout and original illustrations © Coordination Group Publications Ltd. (CGP) 2010
All rights reserved.

How to Use this Book

1

How to Use this Book

This guide is for anyone studying the <u>Relationships</u> section of the AQA English Literature <u>Poetry Anthology</u>. You'll have to either answer an <u>exam question</u> on the poems, or write about them for your <u>controlled assessment</u> — your teacher will tell you which.

Sections One and Two are About The Poems

There are usually <u>two pages</u> about <u>each poem</u>. This is what the pages look like:

There's a nice picture of <u>the poet</u> and some info about their life.

Important or tricky bits of the poem are <u>highlighted</u> and <u>explained</u>.

Difficult words are defined in the <u>poem dictionary</u>.

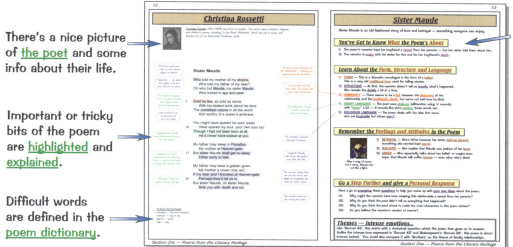

On the right-hand page there are <u>notes</u> about the poem. They include:

- <u>what happens</u> in the poem
- the <u>form</u>, <u>structure</u> and <u>language</u> the poet uses
- the <u>feelings</u> and <u>attitudes</u> in the poem
- a few questions asking you about <u>your feelings</u> on the poem.

If the poem's a bit of a <u>long one</u>, it'll be spread over <u>two pages</u>. One of these will be a <u>pull-out flap</u>. Don't panic. There are full instructions on what to do:

 THIS IS A FLAP. FOLD THIS PAGE OUT.

It's Really Important You Know Your Stuff

Whether you're doing the exam or the controlled assessment, you need to be really <u>familiar</u> with the poems.

1) You <u>won't notice</u> everything about a poem on <u>first reading</u>. Keep reading these poems over and over and <u>over again</u>.

2) If you notice something about a poem then <u>jot it down</u> — there's <u>no limit</u> to the number of <u>good points</u> that could be made about these poems.

3) Make sure you have a go at <u>answering</u> those questions at the bottom of the right-hand page.

Nigel's first response to the poems wasn't all that positive.

The questions are designed to make you <u>think for yourself</u> about the poems. You'll get <u>marks</u> in both the exam and the controlled assessment for giving <u>your own ideas</u> and <u>opinions</u> on the texts — it's called a <u>personal response</u>.

How to Use this Book

How to Use this Book

You've got to make comparisons between the poems in your writing — so I've included two dead handy sections showing their similarities and differences. No need to thank me.

Section Three is About Themes and Ideas

This section will help you make links between the themes presented in the poems — it'll give you loads of ideas of what to write about in your exam or controlled assessment.

A different theme is looked at on each page.

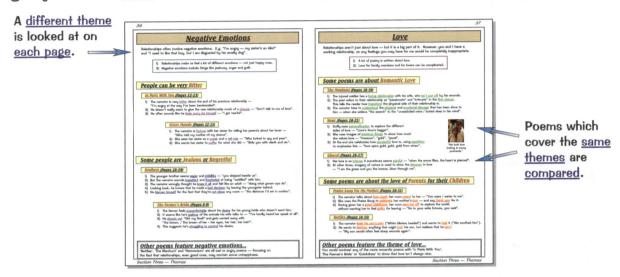

Poems which cover the same themes are compared.

Section Four is About Poetry Techniques

1) This section is all about form, structure and language.
2) It looks at how different poets use features like rhyme, rhythm and imagery to create effects — it's something the examiners are dead keen for you to understand and write about.

Each term is explained...

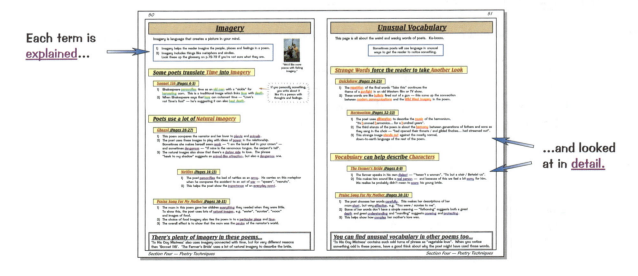

...and looked at in detail.

How to Use this Book

How to Use this Book

If you're studying these poems for the Unit 2 exam, then you need Section Five.
If you're doing these poems for your Unit 5 controlled assessment, look at Section Six.

Section Five Tells You What to Do in Your Exam

This is where you can find out exactly what's involved in your Unit 2: Poetry Across Time exam.

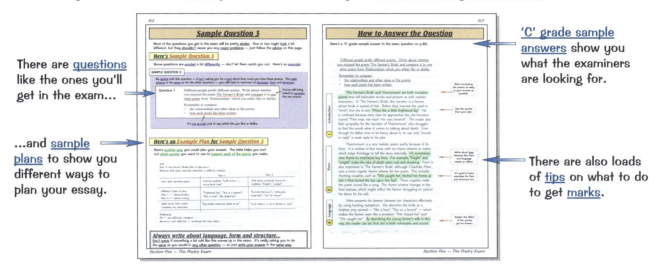

There are questions like the ones you'll get in the exam...

...and sample plans to show you different ways to plan your essay.

'C' grade sample answers show you what the examiners are looking for.

There are also loads of tips on what to do to get marks.

Section Six Tells You What to Do in Your Controlled Assessment

This section gives you the lowdown on the Unit 5: Exploring Poetry controlled assessment.

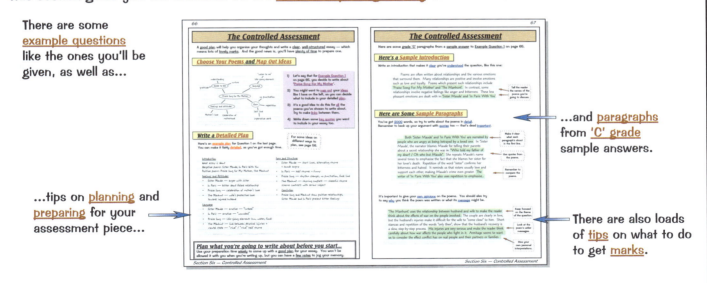

There are some example questions like the ones you'll be given, as well as...

...tips on planning and preparing for your assessment piece...

...and paragraphs from 'C' grade sample answers.

There are also loads of tips on what to do to get marks.

Section Seven Helps You Improve Your Writing Skills

1) This section gives you some great tips on how to answer the question well.
2) There are some useful pointers for writing a good essay too — including advice on quoting and paragraphs. You'll find it dead helpful.

How to Use this Book

William Shakespeare

William Shakespeare (1564-1616) was a successful playwright and poet. He was born in Stratford-upon-Avon, Warwickshire, but lived in London for most of his life. This sonnet is the 116th in a series of 154 on the theme of love.

Sonnet 116

Let me not to the marriage of true minds
Admit impediments; love is not love
Which alters when it alteration finds,
Or bends with the remover to remove.
5 O no it is an ever-fixed mark,
That looks on tempests and is never shaken;
It is the star to every wand'ring bark,
Whose worth's unknown, although his height be taken.
Love's not Time's fool, though rosy lips and cheeks
10 Within his bending sickle's compass come;
Love alters not with his brief hours and weeks,
But bears it out even to the edge of doom.
If this be error and upon me proved,
I never writ, nor no man ever loved.

Annotations (left):
- He believes that nothing can stop true love from lasting.
- Impediments is a word used in marriage services — it reminds us of weddings.
- This metaphor compares love to the Pole Star which doesn't move and helps sailors to navigate.
- Time can take away youth and beauty.
- "I promise this is true."

Annotations (right):
- True love doesn't change even in difficult situations.
- Love is constant — it won't change the way appearances do.
- The star's height can be calculated, but its value to the ships can't be measured.
- Time is personified, which makes the battle between time and love dramatic.
- Any measure of time is short for love, because love lasts till the end of time.

POEM DICTIONARY
impediment — something that stops something or holds it up
bark — small ship with sails
tempests — storms
sickle — a sharp, curved tool for cutting corn always used on pictures of Old Father Time and Death
compass — reach
doom — doomsday: the very last day at the end of the world

Sonnet 116

Shakespeare argues that no matter what happens, true love won't change. Isn't that nice.

You've Got to Know What the Poem's About

1) Shakespeare is writing about how constant true love is.
2) If it really is love, then it doesn't change when circumstances change.
3) He says that if what he says isn't true, then he never wrote anything and no man has ever been in love. Since we know he did write, and men do love, he's saying his words on love are true.

Learn About the Form, Structure and Language

1) FORM — This poem is a sonnet. Sonnets were popular in Shakespeare's day and they were often used for writing about love. It ends with a rhyming couplet.
2) STRUCTURE — The poet uses different images to talk about one idea — that love doesn't change. He ends with a guarantee that he's telling the truth.
3) LANGUAGE ABOUT SAILING — True love is shown as reliable — it guides us in an uncertain world.
4) LANGUAGE ABOUT TIME AND AGEING — When we get older we look different, but true love isn't bothered about the effects of time.

Sonnets are poems with 14 lines. They usually rhyme.

Remember the Feelings and Attitudes in the Poem

"It's all done with satellites now."

1) DEVOTION — The voice in the poem is talking about a love which will not change.
2) CONSTANCY — He sees love as something which won't change even when the person he loves changes.
3) TRUE LOVE — It's not shallow or based on what the loved one looks like.

Go a Step Further and give a Personal Response

Have a go at answering these questions to help you come up with your own ideas about the poem:
Q1. Do you think Shakespeare is writing about the love of younger or older people? Why?
Q2. Can you give this poem a title which you think sums up the ideas in it?
Q3. Would you say this is a poem about love in general, or a love poem to someone in particular?

Themes — attitudes towards love...

Like 'Sonnet 43', this poem deals with an ideal version of what love should be like. You could also compare it with 'To His Coy Mistress', which also deals with the idea of the effects of ageing on love.

Section One — Poems from the Literary Heritage

THIS IS A FLAP.
FOLD THIS PAGE OUT.

To His Coy Mistress

In this poem the narrator is trying to get his mistress to go to bed with him — how romantic.

You've Got to Know What the Poem's About

1) The narrator is telling the woman he loves that she shouldn't play hard to get — there isn't time.
2) He says they should enjoy each other whilst they are still young and attractive.
3) He tries lots of different arguments to persuade her.

Learn About the Form, Structure and Language

1) **FORM** — This poem has a first person narrator. It's made up of rhyming couplets which make the poem sound witty.
2) **STRUCTURE** — In the first stanza the narrator explains that he would like to spend a long time flirting with her, but in the second he says he can't because they won't live forever. In the third stanza he suggests they should get together while they can.
3) **HYPERBOLE** — He makes fun of his mistress's romantic ideas of love using exaggeration.
4) **LANGUAGE ABOUT DEATH** — He reminds his mistress that time is passing — one day they will both be dead.
5) **AGGRESSIVE LANGUAGE** — As the poem goes on he becomes more direct and forceful. He uses passionate and violent imagery.

"First person" means the poet uses words like "I" and "me".

Remember the Feelings and Attitudes in the Poem

Sorry love — you're just not my type.

1) **IMPATIENCE** — He doesn't want to wait a long time for her.
2) **URGENCY** — Time is moving on and he feels that they need to enjoy being together now.
3) **RELUCTANCE** — From the increasing frustration he shows, it appears she doesn't want to have sex with him.

Go a Step Further and give a Personal Response

Have a go at answering these questions to help you come up with your own ideas about the poem:

Q1. How much do we find out about the mistress and her thoughts and feelings?
Q2. Do you think his mistress is really shy, or is she just playing hard to get?
Q3. Some people argue that the narrator of the poem is losing his temper, others that he is making a well-ordered argument. What do you think?

Themes — the passage of time and how it affects people...

The effects of time and death are also discussed in 'Sonnet 116' and 'Sonnet 43'.
The role of lust and physical love is also a theme in 'Hour' and 'In Paris with You'.

Section One — Poems from the Literary Heritage

THIS IS A FLAP.
FOLD THIS PAGE OUT.

The Farmer's Bride

This poem tells the unhappy story of a farmer and his wife.

You've Got to Know What the Poem's About

1) A farmer has been married for three years, but his bride is still frightened of him.
2) He tells the story of how the relationship went wrong. He doesn't blame himself. He desires his wife.
3) He finds her rejection almost unbearable, but he sounds fairly matter-of-fact about it. By the end he seems to be struggling to resist taking her by force.

Learn About the Form, Structure and Language

1) **FORM** — The poem is a dramatic monologue. It has a strong rhythm that keeps the narrative moving forward.
2) **STRUCTURE** — The farmer tells the story of the marriage through the first two stanzas, then goes on to discuss how his wife is now and how he feels towards her.
3) **LANGUAGE ABOUT NATURE** — The farmer uses a lot of imagery from the natural world. He makes his wife sound like a hunted animal.
4) **DIALECT** — The poem contains some dialect words — these tell us a bit about who the farmer is. This adds to the drama because it helps us picture the people involved.

A dramatic monologue is a poem where one person talks about their feelings.

Dialect is a variation in how people speak.

Remember the Feelings and Attitudes in the Poem

"Maybe you should just talk to the guy — tell him how you feel."

1) **FRUSTRATION** — He wants to have a sexual relationship with her and to have children but she's unwilling.
2) **DESIRE** — The farmer is attracted to his wife. We can tell this from the images he uses to describe her and the way he breaks down at the end of the poem.
3) **FEAR** — His wife is afraid of him.

Go a Step Further and give a Personal Response

Have a go at answering these questions to help you come up with your own ideas about the poem:

Q1. How much do you blame the farmer for his wife's attitude?
Q2. Would you describe 'The Farmer's Bride' as a love poem?
Q3. Can you write an ending to this story? What happens next?

Themes — unhappy love...

You could compare this poem with either 'Hour' or 'In Paris With You' which give more modern accounts of how love can be an intense experience. Both this poem and 'To His Coy Mistress' have a frustrated narrator, but this is more tragic whereas the other is funnier.

Section One — Poems from the Literary Heritage

Elizabeth Barrett Browning

Elizabeth Barrett Browning (1806-1861) was born into an affluent family in County Durham. A successful poet in her own right, she was influenced heavily by the poetry of her husband, Robert Browning.

Sonnet 43

How do I love thee? Let me count the ways! —
I love thee to the depth and breadth and height
My soul can reach, when feeling out of sight
For the ends of Being and Ideal Grace.
5 I love thee to the level of everyday's
Most quiet need, by sun and candlelight —
I love thee freely, as men strive for Right, —
I love thee purely, as they turn from Praise;
I love thee with the passion, put to use
10 In my old griefs, ... and with my childhood's faith:
I love thee with the love I seemed to lose
With my lost Saints, — I love thee with the breath,
Smiles, tears, of all my life! — and, if God choose,
I shall but love thee better after death.

Annotations:
- She's talking directly to her husband. It makes the poem more personal.
- "as much as I need anything"
- Each repetition is followed by a different idea — showing how her love has many different sides to it.
- She's committed to him in the same way she used to be committed to religion.
- Her love affects her whole life — it isn't just about the good times.
- She repeats things to make it clear how much she loves him.
- Religious ideas and imagery — her love gives her a spiritual feeling.
- Day and night — her love is timeless.
- She loves without expecting anything in return.
- She thinks her love is good and pure.
- Links her love to the idea of heaven to show how great it is.

POEM DICTIONARY
breadth — width
strive — try hard

Section One — Poems from the Literary Heritage

Sonnet 43

This poem mixes a declaration of love up with a lot of religious imagery — it's a heady brew.

You've Got to Know What the Poem's About

1) This is a love poem, where the poet expresses her love for her lover, Robert Browning.
2) She loves him so much that she sees their love as spiritual and sacred. She counts all of the different ways in which she loves him.
3) Her love is so great that she believes she will love him even after death.

Learn About the Form, Structure and Language

Sonnets are poems with 14 lines. They usually rhyme.

1) FORM — This poem is a sonnet. Sonnets were often used for writing about love.
2) STRUCTURE — The first eight lines give the theme of the poem — comparing the poet's love to religious ideas. The next six lines develop this theme by comparing the strength of her feelings for her lover and the kinds of love she felt as a child.
3) REPETITION — Using the same words repeatedly at the start of phrases is called anaphora. It's often used in the Bible. It makes her poem seem like a prayer.
4) RELIGIOUS LANGUAGE — Her love seems like a religion to her because it gives meaning to her life. Her love is unconditional in the same way religious faith should be.

Remember the Feelings and Attitudes in the Poem

Sonnet 44 — "I love thee more than doughnuts..."

1) DEEP AND LASTING LOVE — The poet uses the strength of spiritual love to emphasise how strongly she feels about her husband.
2) UNSELFISH LOVE — She asks for nothing in return.
3) VIRTUE — The poem makes her love seem morally right.

Go a Step Further and give a Personal Response

Have a go at answering these questions to help you come up with your own ideas about the poem:

Q1. What title might you give this sonnet?
Q2. How realistic do you think this expression of love is?
Q3. How would you describe the character of the narrator?

Themes — love after death...

This poem is about the possibility of such an intense love that it lasts beyond the grave, which is the exact opposite message to the one in 'To His Coy Mistress'. 'Sonnet 43' also picks out different aspects of the narrator's love in a way that you could compare with 'Ghazal'.

Section One — Poems from the Literary Heritage

Christina Rossetti

Christina Rossetti (1830-1894) was born in London. She wrote many romantic, religious and children's poems, including 'In the Bleak Midwinter', which was set to music and became one of our best-loved Christmas carols.

Sister Maude

Who told my mother of my shame,
    Who told my father of my dear?
Oh who but Maude, my sister Maude,
    Who lurked to spy and peer.

5 Cold he lies, as cold as stone,
    With his clotted curls about his face:
The comeliest corpse in all the world
    And worthy of a queen's embrace.

You might have spared his soul, sister,
10   Have spared my soul, your own soul too:
Though I had not been born at all,
    He'd never have looked at you.

My father may sleep in Paradise,
    My mother at Heaven-gate:
15 But sister Maude shall get no sleep
    Either early or late.

My father may wear a golden gown,
    My mother a crown may win;
If my dear and I knocked at Heaven-gate
20   Perhaps they'd let us in:
But sister Maude, oh sister Maude,
    Bide *you* with death and sin.

Annotations:

- Rhetorical questions — the narrator doesn't expect an answer.
- Repetition — she wants the reader to be sure that Maude's to blame.
- This negative language turns us against Maude and makes us feel sorry for the narrator.
- Her boyfriend was handsome, but now he's dead.
- Suggests that Maude told their parents because she was jealous.
- Repetition of "sister" emphasises how close they were — and so how badly betrayed the narrator feels.
- Alliteration helps link sister Maude with sin.
- She doesn't seem ashamed of the relationship — perhaps her parents think she should be.
- It's not clear how her lover died. This makes the poem seem mysterious.
- The alliteration of hard 'c' sounds makes the poem sound angry.
- The narrator's parents may get to heaven.
- Suggests Maude will always feel guilty, even after she dies.
- The narrator thinks that her and her lover's sins might be forgivable, but that her sister's aren't.
- The narrator seems to be cursing her sister.

POEM DICTIONARY
comeliest — the most attractive
embrace — hug or kiss
spared — saved
bide — stay

Section One — Poems from the Literary Heritage

Sister Maude

Sister Maude is an old fashioned story of love and betrayal — something everyone can enjoy.

You've Got to Know What the Poem's About

1) The poem's narrator kept her boyfriend a secret from her parents — but her sister told them about him.
2) The narrator is angry with her sister for this and for her boyfriend's death.

Learn About the Form, Structure and Language

1) FORM — This is a dramatic monologue in the form of a ballad. This is a very old traditional form used for telling stories.
2) STRUCTURE — At first, the narrator doesn't tell us exactly what's happened. She reveals the details a bit at a time.
3) AMBIGUITY — There seems to be a link between the discovery of the relationship and the boyfriend's death, but we're not told how he died.
4) ANGRY LANGUAGE — The poet uses sibilance (alliteration using 's' sounds) with "sister" a lot — it sounds like she's spitting these words out.
5) RELIGIOUS LANGUAGE — The poem deals with the idea that some sins are forgivable but others aren't.

Remember the Feelings and Attitudes in the Poem

After a mug of cocoa and a story, Maude was out like a light.

1) BETRAYAL — She's bitter because her sister told her parents something she wanted kept secret.
2) JEALOUSY — She implies that Maude was jealous of her lover.
3) ANGER — She repeatedly talks about her belief, or maybe even hope, that Maude will suffer forever — even when she's dead.

Go a Step Further and give a Personal Response

Have a go at answering these questions to help you come up with your own ideas about the poem:

Q1. Why might the narrator have been keeping this relationship a secret from her parents?
Q2. Why do you think the poet didn't tell us everything that happened?
Q3. Why do you think the poet chose to make the main characters in this poem sisters?
Q4. Do you believe the narrator's version of events?

Themes — intense emotions...

Like 'Sonnet 43', this starts with a rhetorical question which the poem then goes on to answer. Unlike the intense love expressed in 'Sonnet 43' and Shakespeare's 'Sonnet 116', this poem is about intense hatred. You could also compare it with 'Brothers' on the theme of family relationships.

Section One — Poems from the Literary Heritage

Vernon Scannell

Vernon Scannell (1922-2007) was born in Lincolnshire but moved frequently during his childhood. After a stint in the army, he became a professional boxer and then an English teacher. Many of his poems were shaped by his wartime experience.

Personification is where you describe something as a person with real thoughts and feelings.

Nettles

My son aged three fell in the nettle bed.
'Bed' seemed a curious name for those green spears,
That regiment of spite behind the shed:
It was no place for rest. With sobs and tears
5 The boy came seeking comfort and I saw
White blisters beaded on his tender skin.
We soothed him till his pain was not so raw.
At last he offered us a watery grin,
And then I took my hook and honed the blade
10 And went outside and slashed in fury with it
Till not a nettle in that fierce parade
Stood upright any more. Next task: I lit
A funeral pyre to burn the fallen dead.
But in two weeks the busy sun and rain
15 Had called up tall recruits behind the shed:
My son would often feel sharp wounds again.

Annotations:
- Suggests comfort and safety — so he sees this as an ironic term.
- Personification of the nettles makes them sound like an evil army.
- Describing his careful preparation and then his furious attacks makes his mixed emotions clear.
- More military language. It seems there will always be more nettles to replace the ones he kills.
- The first line is a matter-of-fact description of what happens. This makes it seem more real.
- A weapon with a sharp point as well as the stalk of a plant.
- Here the poem focuses on the boy's pain.
- He can't take away the pain entirely.
- The nettles are like soldiers killed in battle.
- This suggests physical wounds and also emotional pain.

POEM DICTIONARY
honed — sharpened
pyre — a pile of wood for burning dead bodies

Section One — Poems from the Literary Heritage

Nettles

This poem seems to be a simple story about a father's love for his son — but by the end we realise it's also about the pain of trying to look after children.

You've Got to Know What the Poem's About

1) A three-year-old boy falls into a bed of nettles and is badly stung.
2) His father comforts him, then goes out and cuts down the nettles.
3) Two weeks later the nettles have grown back.
4) The story is used to show how parents can't always protect their children from pain.

Learn About the Form, Structure and Language

1) FORM — This is a narrative poem — it tells a story. The poet uses a first person narrator to talk about personal experiences.
2) STRUCTURE — The poem goes through the story in a simple way. He describes things in the order they happened, like a normal story.
3) MILITARY LANGUAGE — Imagery of war is used. The nettles are like vicious soldiers who attack the boy.
4) PAINFUL LANGUAGE — The narrator clearly describes the boy's pain, but also links this to the more general pains of growing up.

Remember the Feelings and Attitudes in the Poem

Q7. What kind of plant is this? (2 marks)

1) ANGER — The father's angry at the nettles which hurt his son.
2) REVENGE — He attacks the nettles and tries to destroy them.
3) TENDERNESS — He takes care of his son and tries to make him feel better.
4) HELPLESSNESS — He can't get rid of the nettles permanently, or stop all the other things that will cause his son pain as he grows.

Go a Step Further and give a Personal Response

Have a go at answering these questions to help you come up with your own ideas about the poem:

Q1. Why do you think the poet tells us the age of his son?
Q2. Why does the poet include details such as that the nettles are behind the shed, and that he used a hook to cut them down?
Q3. What does this poem make you think being a parent is like?

Themes — feelings about loved ones...

Like 'Born Yesterday', this poem talks about the hopes and fears that adults have for young children. As in 'Sister Maude' there is an angry feel to the poem.

Section One — Poems from the Literary Heritage

Philip Larkin

Philip Larkin (1922-1985) was born in Coventry. After graduating from Oxford he spent thirty years working as a librarian for the University of Hull. In 2008 he was named by The Times newspaper as England's best post-war writer.

Born Yesterday

for Sally Amis

> Tightly-folded bud,
> I have wished you something
> None of the others would:
> Not the usual stuff
> 5 About being beautiful,
> Or running off a spring
> Of innocence and love –
> They will all wish you that,
> And should it prove possible,
> 10 Well, you're a lucky girl.
>
> But if it shouldn't, then
> May you be ordinary;
> Have, like other women,
> An average of talents:
> 15 Not ugly, not good-looking,
> Nothing uncustomary
> To pull you off your balance,
> That, unworkable itself,
> Stops all the rest from working.
> 20 In fact, may you be dull –
> If that is what a skilled,
> Vigilant, flexible,
> Unemphasised, enthralled
> Catching of happiness is called.

Annotations:
- New life, ready to blossom.
- His wish is going to be different from the others.
- He doubts whether these wishes will really come true.
- He doesn't want her to have anything that makes her stand out.
- If you have an extreme characteristic, it will spread to stop everything else from working.
- These five adjectives show how complicated catching happiness is.
- This image is affectionate — it seems to contrast with the hope that she isn't beautiful.
- It sounds like the usual things people wish for a baby aren't very helpful.
- A source of pure, unpolluted water.
- At first his 'unexciting' wishes seem unkind.
- He explains how being dull is more valuable than any of the 'virtues' in the first stanza.
- Making the last two lines rhyme means they stand out from the rest of the poem.

POEM DICTIONARY
uncustomary — unusual
Vigilant — alert, watchful
enthralled — fascinated

Section One — Poems from the Literary Heritage

Born Yesterday

This poem is about what it really takes to be happy — and it may not be quite what you'd expect from a poet.

You've Got to Know What the Poem's About

1) Larkin wrote this poem the day after the birth of Sally Amis, daughter of his friend Kingsley Amis.
2) He takes the fairy-tale idea of giving out wishes to a newborn, but adds a twist to it — his wish is not for great beauty and exciting things. Instead he wants her to have more practical, useful talents.

If he was any more attractive, he'd fall off.

Learn About the Form, Structure and Language

1) FORM — The lack of rhyme makes most of the poem seem more like normal spoken English, and puts extra emphasis on the rhyming couplet at the end.
2) STRUCTURE — The poet starts off talking about the so-called gifts or virtues that most people would wish for a newborn with an ironic tone. The second stanza is more direct and deals with the real things that are needed to be happy.
3) CYNICAL LANGUAGE — The poet sounds sceptical when he describes what extraordinary gifts are worth.
4) LANGUAGE ABOUT ORDINARINESS — The poet gives an unexciting description of his hopes. But he then surprises us with a statement of how important and how special that kind of ordinariness is.

Remember the Feelings and Attitudes in the Poem

1) TENDERNESS — He expresses genuine good feelings for his friend's newborn baby daughter.
2) SCORN — He's quite cruel about the traditional, fairy-tale kind of wishes people make for babies.
3) REALISM — He gives a down-to-earth view of the way people can achieve happiness.

Go a Step Further and give a Personal Response

Have a go at answering these questions to help you come up with your own ideas about the poem:

Q1. What impact does the title have on the meaning of the poem?
Q2. How far do you agree with Larkin's wishes?
Q3. Many of the poems in this book express how important love is — how is this poem different?

Themes — what's important...

This message links with the ideas of Shakespeare in 'Sonnet 116', that the usual poetic stuff which celebrates beauty isn't what's really important. Both this poem and 'To His Coy Mistress' talk about the values of others as being unrealistic, wishful thinking.

Section One — Poems from the Literary Heritage

Simon Armitage

Simon Armitage was born in 1963 in West Yorkshire. As well as poetry, he's also written four stage plays, and writes for TV, film and radio. He studied geography in Portsmouth, and he's now a Senior Lecturer in Creative Writing at Manchester Metropolitan University.

The Manhunt

After the first phase,
after passionate nights and intimate days,

only then would he let me trace
the frozen river which ran through his face,

5   only then would he let me explore
the blown hinge of his lower jaw,

and handle and hold
the damaged, porcelain collar-bone,

and mind and attend
10 the fractured rudder of shoulder-blade,

and finger and thumb
the parachute silk of his punctured lung.

Only then could I bind the struts
and climb the rungs of his broken ribs,

15 and feel the hurt
of his grazed heart.

Skirting along,
only then could I picture the scan,

the foetus of metal beneath his chest
20 where the bullet had finally come to rest.

Then I widened the search,
traced the scarring back to its source

to a sweating, unexploded mine
buried deep in his mind, around which

25 every nerve in his body had tightened and closed.
Then, and only then, did I come close.

Annotations:
- Sounds like a normal love poem — describing the first stages of a new relationship.
- Suggests she is slowly overcoming his resistance.
- Repetition suggests this is a slow, painful process.
- References to scarring, but it doesn't stop her from loving him.
- Emphasises how fragile he is and how careful she has to be with him.
- The repetition of this sentence structure with two verbs emphasises that this is an active process.
- Suggests she's patching him up — as if tying his broken ribs back in place.
- Parachutes are used by the army. A damaged one would be useless.
- Consonance (repetition of the 'h') emphasises his emotional pain.
- This makes it sound like she's climbed inside him.
- She is imagining the scan being like one for a baby.
- His memories make him tense and stressed — they're buried but they might still 'explode'.
- His main problems are psychological and emotional.
- This a muted ending — he's not all better.
- Ambiguity — she had to wait until now to get 'close' to him, but she's still only "come close".

POEM DICTIONARY
struts — lengths of wood or metal that strengthen a framework
rudder — a device attached to the underside of a boat used for steering

The Manhunt

This poem shows how the damage war does continues long after the conflict is over.

You've Got to Know What the Poem's About

1) It's written as if spoken by the wife of a soldier. The soldier has come home from war with serious gun shot wounds.
2) More difficult to see and understand are the mental scars his experiences have left him with and the problems these are causing.

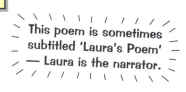
This poem is sometimes subtitled 'Laura's Poem' — Laura is the narrator.

Learn About the Form, Structure and Language

1) FORM — This is a first-person narrative from Laura's viewpoint. The poem is divided into couplets — these emphasise that Laura is describing a slow, step-by-step process.
2) STRUCTURE — Different injuries are introduced in different couplets — the reader explores the husband's body and mind in the same slow way his wife has done.
3) LANGUAGE ABOUT THE BODY — The husband's body is described using a range of different adjectives that describe damage. These are paired with metaphors that suggest his body has become a group of broken objects.
4) LANGUAGE ABOUT CARING — The poet employs a range of different verbs describing how the woman is caring for the injured man.

A couplet is a pair of lines that are next to each other.

Remember the Feelings and Attitudes in the Poem

1) CARING — She is sensitive in her approach to her wounded husband.
2) PATIENCE — It takes the whole poem for the woman to "come close" to her husband.
3) PAIN — The words used to describe the man suggest that his experiences have hurt him mentally and physically.

Go a Step Further and give a Personal Response

Have a go at answering these questions to help you come up with your own ideas about the poem:

Q1. Why do you think the poet has called this poem 'The Manhunt'?
Q2. How are the details in this poem different to the ones in a news story or a film about war?
Q3. How does this poem make you feel about war? Why?

Themes — pain and suffering...

You could compare this poem to 'Nettles' — they're both on the theme of how people respond to the suffering of a loved one. This poem also gives an example of love continuing in difficult times, which is like the ideal of love in Shakespeare's 'Sonnet 116'.

Section Two — Contemporary Poems

Carol Ann Duffy

Carol Ann Duffy was born in 1955 in Glasgow. She studied philosophy at the University of Liverpool, and in 1996 began lecturing in poetry at Manchester Metropolitan University. As well as writing poetry, she has also written plays. In 2009 she became the Poet Laureate.

Hour

Love's time's beggar, but even a single hour,
bright as a dropped coin, makes love rich.
We find an hour together, spend it not on flowers
or wine, but the whole of the summer sky and a grass ditch.

5 For thousands of seconds we kiss; your hair
like treasure on the ground; the Midas light
turning your limbs to gold. Time slows, for here
we are millionaires, backhanding the night

so nothing dark will end our shining hour,
10 no jewel hold a candle to the cuckoo spit
hung from the blade of grass at your ear,
no chandelier or spotlight see you better lit

than here. Now. Time hates love, wants love poor,
but love spins gold, gold, gold from straw.

Annotations:
- Time together is a valuable gift.
- Love needs time, but time doesn't need love.
- Gives the sense of time slowing down.
- The light at sunset makes everything look golden — just like love makes everything look different.
- This might mean bribing the night to stay away.
- They are rich because they have so much love.
- If you're in love, everything seems precious.
- Repetition — this emphasises how wonderful this time is.
- This one-word sentence stands out. The poet wants us to focus on the moment.
- This is what Rumpelstiltskin does in the fairy tale.
- Making something precious from something ordinary makes it seem like magic.

POEM DICTIONARY
Midas — Mythical ancient Greek king who turned everything he touched into gold
cuckoo spit — white froth found on plants produced by bugs

Hour

This poem is about how precious time is for lovers.

You've Got to Know What the Poem's About

1) This poem describes an hour spent between the narrator and her lover.
2) The poet personifies time as love's enemy. Love almost manages to make time stand still.

Learn About the Form, Structure and Language

1) FORM — This poem has 14 lines and it rhymes — a bit like a Shakespearean love sonnet. Unlike a sonnet though, it has an irregular rhythm. The narrator is talking directly to her lover, which makes it seem intimate.
2) STRUCTURE — The poem starts off with two lines on the personification of love and time. The final couplet links back to the personified images of time and love in the first stanza.
3) LANGUAGE ABOUT TIME — Time is shown as the enemy of love.
4) LANGUAGE ABOUT MONEY AND WEALTH — The poem plays with ideas about the value of money compared to time spent together.

Personification is where you write about something as if it's a person with thoughts and feelings.

Remember the Feelings and Attitudes in the Poem

1) CHERISHING THE MOMENT — Love is felt to be precious and valuable.
2) STRONG BELIEF — The poem believes love isn't affected by time.
3) PHYSICAL PLEASURE — Love is not just an idea, it's real and physical — like lying in a ditch, kissing.

"Isn't it time you two got a room?"

Go a Step Further and give a Personal Response

Have a go at answering these questions to help you come up with your own ideas about the poem:

Q1. Why do you think the poet uses personification in the poem?
Q2. Why do you think the poet wrote this poem as a type of sonnet?

Themes — love against time...

'Sonnet 116' deals with the relationship between time and love, and also uses personification to do so. Another poem that has time as the enemy of love is 'To His Coy Mistress'. You could also compare this poem to 'Sonnet 43' on the theme of the value of love.

Section Two — Contemporary Poems

James Fenton

James Fenton was born in 1949 in Lincoln. He studied at Magdalen College, Oxford, after which he travelled to East Asia and worked as a political journalist and war correspondent. In 2007 he was awarded the Queen's Gold Medal for Poetry.

In Paris With You

Don't talk to me of love. I've had an earful
And I get tearful when I've downed a drink or two.
I'm one of your talking wounded.
I'm a hostage. I'm maroonded.
5   But I'm in Paris with you.

Yes I'm angry at the way I've been bamboozled
And resentful at the mess I've been through.
I admit I'm on the rebound
And I don't care where are *we* bound.
10 I'm in Paris with you.

Do you mind if we do *not* go to the Louvre,
If we say sod off to sodding Notre Dame,
If we skip the Champs Elysées
And remain here in this sleazy
15 Old hotel room
Doing this and that
To what and whom
Learning who you are,
Learning what I am.

20 Don't talk to me of love. Let's talk of Paris,
The little bit of Paris in our view.
There's that crack across the ceiling
And the hotel walls are peeling
And I'm in Paris with you.

25 Don't talk to me of love. Let's talk of Paris.
I'm in Paris with the slightest thing you do.
I'm in Paris with your eyes, your mouth,
I'm in Paris with… all points south.
Am I embarrassing you?
30 I'm in Paris with you.

Section Two — Contemporary Poems

In Paris With You

Paris — city of romance, city of lovers... um, not in this case...

You've Got to Know What the Poem's About

1) The speaker in the poem is upset about love. He's split up with somebody and sees himself as a victim.
2) He's gone to Paris with someone else, but still seems unhappy.
   He doesn't want to go out into the city — he'd rather stay in the hotel room.

Learn About the Form, Structure and Language

1) FORM — The third stanza is very different to the rest, which makes it stand out.
   The poem is structured like a song, with lots of repetition and internal rhymes.
2) STRUCTURE — The first two stanzas are about the narrator, the next few are about Paris.
   The third stanza is structured differently. This is where he tells his lover what he wants.
3) LANGUAGE ABOUT PARIS — The idea of being in Paris is very important. Paris is known as the city of love — but in this case it seems ironic because his thoughts aren't very romantic.
4) HUMOROUS LANGUAGE — Nearly every stanza contains an unexpected rhyme. He also keeps repeating the word Paris, but he only really talks about the grotty hotel room.

Remember the Feelings and Attitudes in the Poem

1) SELF PITY — He starts the poem feeling sorry for himself.
2) BITTERNESS — He's angry about the end of his last relationship.
3) HUMOUR — He's self pitying, but the puns and unexpected rhymes suggest humour.
4) LUST — He makes his intentions very clear.

"Sorry — can't be bothered."

Go a Step Further and give a Personal Response

Have a go at answering these questions to help you come up with your own ideas about the poem:

Q1. How would you describe the narrator's mood at the beginning of the poem, and at the end?
Q2. Do you think that this poem is more funny or sad?
Q3. Why do you think the word Paris is repeated so often?

Themes — negative emotions...
The narrator starts this poem very bitterly — you could compare this to the anger in 'Sister Maude' and the feeling of being hurt in 'Quickdraw'. 'To His Coy Mistress' also has a narrator who is trying to seduce someone — and it's another poem that uses humour.

Section Two — Contemporary Poems

Carol Ann Duffy

Carol Ann Duffy was born in 1955 in Glasgow. She studied philosophy at the University of Liverpool, and in 1996 began lecturing in poetry at Manchester Metropolitan University. As well as writing poetry, she has also written plays. In 2009 she became the Poet Laureate.

Quickdraw

> I wear the two, the mobile and the landline phones,
> like guns, slung from the pockets on my hips. I'm all
> alone. You ring, quickdraw, your voice a pellet
> in my ear, and hear me groan.
>
> 5   You've wounded me.
> Next time, you speak after the tone. I twirl the phone,
> then squeeze the trigger of my tongue, wide of the mark.
> You choose your spot, then blast me
>
>   through the heart.
> 10 And this is love, high noon, calamity, hard liquor
> in the old Last Chance saloon. I show the mobile
> to the Sheriff; in my boot, another one's
>
> concealed. You text them both at once. I reel.
> Down on my knees, I fumble for the phone,
> 15 read the silver bullets of your kiss. Take this ...
> and this ... and this ... and this ... and this ...

Annotations:

- *Enjambment makes this word stand out by leaving it alone on the line away from the rest of its sentence.* (→ "alone")
- *She answers the phone quickly.* (→ "quickdraw")
- *Rhyme links this word with "alone" on previous line.* (→ "groan")
- *Split lines show how hurt she is by her lover's words.* (→ "You've wounded me." / "through the heart.")
- *Images from Cowboy and Western films.* (→ "high noon, calamity, hard liquor" / "the old Last Chance saloon")
- *Sounds like the relationship is nearly over.*
- *It's like she's been shot and also links the events with films ('reel' could be a film reel).* (→ "I reel.")
- *Sound precious and valuable.* (→ "silver bullets")
- *These texted kisses are like bullets fired from a gun.* (→ "and this ... and this ...")

POEM DICTIONARY
quickdraw — a game to see who can draw their gun the fastest
high noon — midday. Also the name of a Cowboy and Western film
calamity — disaster. Also the nickname of the famous Wild West woman, 'Calamity Jane'
hard liquor — strong alcohol
Last Chance saloon — a type of American bar. Also a phrase that means, "this is our last chance"
concealed — hidden

Section Two — Contemporary Poems

Quickdraw

This poem is about a difficult relationship — but still a tense and exciting one.

You've Got to Know What the Poem's About

1) This poem compares the phone calls and texts in a relationship to a gun fight in a Western.
2) The narrator always seems to come off worst, and is left hurt and wounded.
3) What finally finishes her off isn't cruelty, but a series of text message kisses which hit her like bullets.

Learn About the Form, Structure and Language

Enjambment is where sentences run over from one line or stanza to the next.

1) **FORM** — This poem uses split lines and enjambment. This adds to the tension as we don't know what to expect next, just as the narrator doesn't.
2) **STRUCTURE** — The poem describes how the lover gets in touch — and how the narrator reacts to this. We experience events in the order the narrator does, adding to the tension.
3) **LANGUAGE ABOUT COMMUNICATION** — The poem talks about phones and texting. This helps the poem to seem modern and different.
4) **LANGUAGE FROM WESTERNS** — The poem has some quite corny imagery taken from TV and cinema. These old-fashioned images contrast with the references to mobile phones and text messaging.

Remember the Feelings and Attitudes in the Poem

"Put your hands up, sweetheart."

1) **HURT** — The Western imagery makes the pain of being in a relationship seem physical — knocking her down in the final stanza.
2) **EXPECTATION** — Despite the pain the relationship is causing her the narrator seems desperate to get the messages.
3) **TENSION** — The narrator seems on edge throughout the poem.

Go a Step Further and give a Personal Response

Have a go at answering these questions to help you come up with your own ideas about the poem:

Q1. Who do you think the Sheriff might be?
Q2. What do you think about the image of kisses being like bullets?

Themes — attitudes towards love...

Sometimes romantic love involves people getting hurt — which is something this poem, 'The Farmer's Bride' and 'In Paris With You' all deal with. You could also talk about the theme of communication in this poem, which is also dealt with, in a very different way, in 'The Manhunt'.

Section Two — Contemporary Poems

Mimi Khalvati

Mimi Khalvati was born in 1944 in Tehran. She went to boarding school on the Isle of Wight, then studied in London. She founded The Poetry School, where she is now a tutor, and has worked as an actor and director in the UK and Iran.

[This isn't just the title, it's the form of the poem.]

Ghazal

If I am the grass and you the breeze, blow through me.
If I am the rose and you the bird, then woo me.

If you are the rhyme and I the refrain, don't hang
on my lips, come and I'll come too when you cue me.

[The enjambment makes it sound like she's waiting.]
[She wants him to be firm but also gentle with her.]

5 If yours is the iron fist in the velvet glove
when the arrow flies, the heart is pierced, tattoo me.

[Lots of people have tattoos of a heart with an arrow through it.]

If mine is the venomous tongue, the serpent's tail,
charmer, use your charm, weave a spell and subdue me.

[She wants him to be like a snake charmer — teasing and in control.]
[She describes herself as a dangerous animal.]

If I am the laurel leaf in your crown, you are
10 the arms around my bark, arms that never knew me.

Oh would that I were bark! So old and still in leaf.
And you, dropping in my shade, dew to bedew me!

[This couplet could be describing the whole poem.]

What shape should I take to marry your own, have you
– hawk to my shadow, moth to my flame – pursue me?

[She wants him to chase after her.]

15 If I rise in the east as you die in the west,
die for my sake, my love, every night renew me.

[Like the sun and moon taking it in turns to rise and set.]

If, when it ends, we are just good friends, be my Friend,
muse, lover and guide, Shamsuddin to my Rumi.

[You wouldn't usually find this idea in a traditional love poem.]

Be heaven and earth to me and I'll be twice the me
20 I am, if only half the world you are to me.

[This type of poem usually has the poet's name in the last stanza — "twice the me" is Mimi.]

POEM DICTIONARY
refrain — a line that is repeated in poetry or song
subdue — quieten down
laurel — laurel leaves in a wreath are traditional symbols of victory
bedew — make something wet — like dew
muse — someone who inspires an artist
Shamsuddin — or Shams Tabrizi, a friend of the poet Rumi
Rumi — important religious figure and poet. He was close friends with Shams (or Shamsuddin) —
    when Shams disappeared Rumi was inspired to write mystical poetry

Section Two — Contemporary Poems

Ghazal

This poem uses a very old form to declare the feelings of the narrator for a loved one.
No one's ever written me a poem.

You've Got to Know What the Poem's About

1) In this poem, the narrator talks about intense feelings of love.
2) She makes up a new image, or a number of images, in each stanza.

Learn About the Form, Structure and Language

1) FORM — This poem is a ghazal. It's an old form of poetry from the Middle East that was often used to talk about love. The final word in each couplet is the same, and the last-but-one words in each stanza rhyme with each other.
2) STRUCTURE — Each stanza is separate from the rest, so we get lots of different images and ideas. This makes this poem appear playful but also quite intense.
3) LANGUAGE ABOUT NATURE — This makes their love seem like a natural thing. It also makes it seem permanent.
4) LANGUAGE ABOUT BEING LOVED — Sometimes this language is quite aggressive — her love isn't all about sweetness.

"If I am the beef, potatoes, carrots and cabbage, and you the simmering stock..."

Remember the Feelings and Attitudes in the Poem

1) INTENSE LOVE — She seems slightly obsessed with her lover.
2) PLAYFULNESS — The different images and repeating rhymes make this seem a happy and playful poem.
3) PLEASURE — The narrator seems to enjoy being in love and the language of love.

Go a Step Further and give a Personal Response

Have a go at answering these questions to help you come up with your own ideas about the poem:
Q1. What title would you give to this ghazal?
Q2. What do you think the poem reveals about the person it was written to?
Q3. Do any of these images make you think that there's a darker side to love? How?

Themes — attitudes towards love...

This poem uses a lot of natural imagery, which you could use to connect it to 'The Farmer's Bride', 'Nettles' and 'Hour'. It has a feeling of lust, so you could compare it to 'To His Coy Mistress' or 'Hour'.

Section Two — Contemporary Poems

Andrew Forster

Andrew Forster was born in South Yorkshire. His first poetry collection, 'Fear of Thunder', was published in 2007.

Brothers

Saddled with you for the afternoon, me and Paul
ambled across the threadbare field to the bus stop,
talking over Sheffield Wednesday's chances in the Cup
while you skipped beside us in your ridiculous tank-top,
5   spouting six-year-old views on Rotherham United.

Suddenly you froze, said you hadn't any bus fare.
I sighed, said you should go and ask Mum
and while you windmilled home I looked at Paul.
His smile, like mine, said I was nine and he was ten
10 and we must stroll the town, doing what grown-ups do.

As a bus crested the hill we chased Olympic Gold.
Looking back I saw you spring towards the gate,
your hand holding out what must have been a coin.
I ran on, unable to close the distance I'd set in motion.

Annotations:
- He's annoyed he's stuck with his little brother.
- He thinks his brother's too young to say anything worthwhile about football.
- Rotherham are a less fashionable club than Sheffield Wednesday.
- Happy image.
- They feel grown up, but actually they're quite young.
- They think they're really mature.
- The older two move more slowly and with confidence.
- Shows they're much faster than their little brother. It's also a kid's game.
- He's now too far away to see.
- It's not clear if he can't or just doesn't want to.
- This event might have made their relationship less close.

POEM DICTIONARY
threadbare — patchy, worn-out
crested — came over the top of

Section Two — Contemporary Poems

Brothers

This is a poem about an event in the narrator's childhood — but it might also be about sibling relationships in general. Personally, I blame the parents.

You've Got to Know What the Poem's About

1) The narrator remembers a moment from his childhood. He and his older brother have to look after their younger brother for the afternoon.
2) They're fed up with him — but excited to be out on their own.
3) They send their younger brother back to get his bus fare from their mum. But then they run off, leaving him behind.

If only she'd remembered to give Timmy his bus fare, this could all have been avoided.

Learn About the Form, Structure and Language

1) FORM — This is a narrative poem. He's talking to the younger brother. It's written in free verse, so it sounds quite natural and chatty.
2) STRUCTURE — The first stanza tells us what the brothers' relationship is like. The second explains how the youngest had to go back. The third stanza describes how he then got left behind.
3) LANGUAGE ABOUT YOUTH — The little boy seems young and excitable. The older brothers think they're grown up, but they still play children's games.
4) LANGUAGE ABOUT MATURITY — The older two think they're mature because they talk and act confidently. But if they were really grown up, they'd look after their brother.

Narrative poems tell a story. Free verse has no regular rhyme or rhythm.

Remember the Feelings and Attitudes in the Poem

1) FRUSTRATION — The older brothers want to get away from their little brother.
2) GUILT — The narrator describes his younger brother as eager and child-like. This makes the narrator's actions seem worse.
3) REGRET — The narrator seems to wish he could go back and change what he did.

Go a Step Further and give a Personal Response

Have a go at answering these questions to help you come up with your own ideas about the poem:

Q1. What would you think about the poem if the younger child was a sister?
Q2. Why do you think the poet chose to call this poem 'Brothers'?
Q3. What does the last line suggest about how the relationship developed after this event?

Themes — family relationships...

This poem is about an unhappy event in the relationship between brothers — for an angrier, more violent version between sisters you could always look at 'Sister Maude'. Like 'Nettles', this is a poem that reflects back on a childhood incident.

Section Two — Contemporary Poems

Grace Nichols

Grace Nichols was born in Guyana in 1950. She was a teacher and journalist in the Caribbean until she moved to Britain in 1977. Both of these cultures are important to her.

Praise Song For My Mother

You were
water to me
deep and bold and fathoming

5   You were
moon's eye to me
pull and grained and mantling

You were
sunrise to me
rise and warm and streaming

10   You were
the fish's red gill to me
the flame tree's spread to me
the crab's leg/the fried plantain smell
    replenishing replenishing

15   Go to your wide futures, you said

Annotations:
- The moon pulls the tides — suggests a natural influence.
- Might suggest flowing water or sunlight.
- Strong image suggests she couldn't breathe without her mother.
- Her mother wanted her to live life to the full.
- Double meaning — suggests both depth and understanding.
- Repetition makes this sound formal — she doesn't want to use everyday spoken English.
- These smells merge into one.
- Repetition shows her mum always did these things for her — it wasn't a one off.

POEM DICTIONARY
fathoming — to get to the bottom of something or to measure the depth of something
grained — textured like the surface of wood
mantling — to cover or wrap up — a mantle is a type of cloak
plantain — a banana-like food from the Caribbean

Section Two — Contemporary Poems

Praise Song For My Mother

This is a poem all about how great someone's mother is. Just think, without Grace Nichols's mum, you'd be looking at a couple of blank pages. Cheers Mrs N.

You've Got to Know What the Poem's About

1) The mum in this poem was the whole world to her child.
2) The narrator compares her mum to water and food — these are things you need to live.
3) She also compares her to the moon and the sun — her mum was as important to her as day and night.

Learn About the Form, Structure and Language

1) FORM — Each of the first three stanzas describes what the mum was like using a different image. Each stanza opens with the same line, which makes it seem lyrical (like the song of the title).
2) STRUCTURE — The poem doesn't have a story or much punctuation — it's like the good memories have merged into one. It also suggests that this poem isn't about a single event, but the experiences of many years.
3) LANGUAGE ABOUT HER MOTHER — The poem has words in it that wouldn't normally be used to describe a loved one — this makes it seem heartfelt. Many of the words don't have one simple meaning — making us see the mother's importance as beyond simple explanations.
4) LANGUAGE ABOUT FOOD — The types of food described are eaten in the Caribbean. This links the mum to a specific place and emphasises how she looked after her children.

Remember the Feelings and Attitudes in the Poem

1) GRATITUDE — The poem is expressing her thanks for her mother's love and support.
2) JOY — The memories she has of her mother are warm and happy ones.
3) PRAISE — This poem gives her the chance to tell everyone how she feels about her mother.

You were chicken burgers to me — thanks Mum.

Go a Step Further and give a Personal Response

Have a go at answering these questions to help you come up with your own ideas about the poem:

Q1. What do you think the image of sunrise suggests about how the narrator sees her mother?
Q2. What can you learn about the mother's feelings for her daughter?
Q3. Why do you think the poet makes food so important in the poem?

Themes — parental love...

You could compare this poem with 'Harmonium', which is also about the narrator's relationship with a parent. 'Nettles' looks at the same theme from the perspective of the parent rather than their child. You could also look at how this poem and 'Ghazal' use natural imagery.

Section Two — Contemporary Poems

Simon Armitage

Simon Armitage was born in 1963 in West Yorkshire. As well as poetry, he's also written four stage plays, and writes for TV, film and radio. He studied geography in Portsmouth, and he's now a Senior Lecturer in Creative Writing at Manchester Metropolitan University.

Harmonium

> The narrator gives us realistic details to suggest this event did actually happen.

> Unused and neglected.

The *Farrand Chapelette* was gathering dust
in the shadowy porch of Marsden Church.
And was due to be bundled off to the skip.
Or was mine, for a song, if I wanted it.

> Pun — he got it cheaply and he can use it for singing.

> Unromantic language — it's being treated like any other rubbish.

5 Sunlight, through stained glass, which day to day
could beatify saints and raise the dead,
had aged the harmonium's softwood case
and yellowed the fingernails of its keys.
And one of its notes had lost its tongue,
10 and holes were worn in both the treadles
where the organist's feet, in grey, woollen socks
and leather-soled shoes, had pedalled and pedalled.

> The church has a holy atmosphere.

> Personifies the harmonium — it's described like an old person.

> Onomatopoeia — this phrase sounds like the noise a harmonium makes.

> Repetition emphasises the passing of time.

But its hummed harmonics still struck a chord:
for a hundred years that organ had stood
15 by the choristers' stalls, where father and son,
each in their time, had opened their throats
and gilded finches — like high notes — had streamed out.

> Pun — it's appealing and can still play chords.

> This lively image stands out from the ordinariness of the rest of the poem.

Through his own blue cloud of tobacco smog,
with smoker's fingers and dottled thumbs,
20 he comes to help me cart it away.
And we carry it flat, laid on its back.
And he, being him, can't help but say
that the next box I'll shoulder through this nave
will bear the freight of his own dead weight.
25 And I, being me, then mouth in reply
some shallow or sorry phrase or word
too starved of breath to make itself heard.

> He's old. His tobacco-stained fingers are linked to the harmonium's yellow keys.

> A body is carried like this in a coffin for a funeral.

> His dad makes a joke about his own funeral.

> Last two lines rhyme for emphasis. The narrator doesn't know what to say after his dad's joke.

POEM DICTIONARY
harmonium — a type of organ which was often found in small churches, operated by pumping two treadles
Farrand Chapelette — the make of the harmonium
Marsden — a village in West Yorkshire
beatify — declare someone's holiness or make very happy
treadle — a lever you work with your foot
gilded — covered with a layer of gold

Section Two — Contemporary Poems

Harmonium

...in which the narrator heads off to a small church to pick up a church organ.
You heard it here first.

You've Got to Know What the Poem's About

1) The narrator and his dad are picking up a harmonium that he's bought cheaply from a church.
2) He thinks about how time has affected the instrument — it's been played in the church for years.
3) His dad is helping him take the harmonium away.
4) His dad makes a joke about death that makes the narrator uncomfortable.

Learn About the Form, Structure and Language

1) FORM — The poem is written in free verse, so it sounds like ordinary speech.
2) STRUCTURE — The poem starts off by explaining how he discovered the harmonium. The second stanza talks about how the harmonium looks now, the third stanza about its past in the church. The last stanza is about the relationship between the narrator and his dad.
3) ORDINARY LANGUAGE — Much of the language is quite unromantic. It sets the scene and contrasts with the spiritual use of the harmonium.
4) LANGUAGE ABOUT TIME — The effects of time are described through the damage to the harmonium. The poem links the harmonium to the dad, who's also getting old.
5) HUMOROUS LANGUAGE — This poem contains a number of puns — jokes with double meanings.

Remember the Feelings and Attitudes in the Poem

1) SPEECHLESSNESS — The narrator feels awkward and doesn't want to talk about his dad's death.
2) HUMOUR — The narrator makes puns about the harmonium and the dad jokes about his own death.
3) SADNESS — The poem deals with the idea of death and the effects of time.

Check out the treadles on this one.

Go a Step Further and give a Personal Response

Have a go at answering these questions to help you come up with your own ideas about the poem:

Q1.   Why does the poet mention his father's fingers and thumbs, and the organist's feet?
Q2.   What does the imagery in line 17 make you think of?
Q3.   Why do you think the narrator wants the harmonium?

Themes — unhappiness...

'Harmonium' deals with how family relationships, even when they're generally good ones, can be a source of unhappiness. Another poem that touches upon a similar theme is 'Nettles', which looks at the father-son relationship from the dad's point of view.

Section Two — Contemporary Poems

SECTION THREE — THEMES

Relationships

All of the poems in this book cover the theme of relationships. In the exam you'll be expected to be able to make links between these poems.

> 1) Relationships are the connections between two or more people.
> 2) There are romantic relationships, family relationships, and the relationships you have with your friends.

People can have Different Feelings about each other

To His Coy Mistress (Pages 6-7)
1) The narrator wants to have a physical relationship with his mistress — "let us sport us while we may" — but she needs persuading.
2) The narrator seems frustrated because she doesn't agree with him.

Somehow they remained great friends — despite having different feelings about skinny dipping.

The Farmer's Bride (Pages 8-9)
1) The farmer wants to be able to touch and love his bride, but she is really scared of him — "'Not near, not near!' her eyes beseech".
2) The farmer fancies her, but he's also sad because she tries to avoid him.
3) She seems to see him only as a threat.

People in a relationship can feel Protective

The Manhunt (Pages 18-19)
1) The ex-soldier's wife isn't put off by her husband's injuries. She wants to "bind the struts" and help him come to terms with what happened to him.
2) She shows love and loyalty by sticking with her husband through difficult times.

Nettles (Pages 14-15)
1) The dad really wants to protect his son, not just from the nettles, which he "slashed in fury", but also from the pains in life.
2) All parents probably feel sad that they can't stop their children being hurt.

Born Yesterday (Pages 16-17)
1) The narrator wants Sally to have the "talents" needed to be happy in life.
2) He says that she needs to be protected from the pressure of being too talented or attractive, because these things can stop you being happy.

There are other poems which touch on these themes...
Differences in feelings can sometimes even lead to aggression — like in the western gunfight-style imagery in 'Quickdraw'. In 'Brothers' the two older brothers feel exasperated with their younger brother, but he seems excited to be out with them.

Relationships

Relationships aren't always about sweetness and light.

Sometimes people can be Mean and Cruel

Sister Maude (Pages 12-13)

1) The narrator wants her sister to suffer for telling her parents about her relationship — "But sister Maude shall get no sleep".
2) She aims to hurt her sister by telling her that the young man would never have fancied her anyway — "He'd never have looked at you".

Quickdraw (Pages 24-25)

1) The bad telephone call and texts from her lover really upset the character in this poem — "You choose your spot, then blast me / through the heart".
2) By making their relationship seem like a gunfight, she shows that relationships can sometimes involve conflict and fighting.

"LOL?" — "LMAO."

Some people are just Inconsiderate

In Paris With You (Pages 22-23)

1) The narrator's so upset about the end of his last relationship, he doesn't care about the feelings of the person he's with now — "I don't care where are *we* bound".
2) His feelings show how a negative end to one relationship can have a bad effect on future relationships.

Brothers (Pages 28-29)

1) The older children don't go back for their younger brother.
2) The narrator knows this was a mean thing to do and hints at how sorry he feels — "I ran on, unable to close the distance I'd set in motion".
3) This shows that the tensions in family relationships often go back to childhood.

> There are a wide range of different relationships in this selection, which cover around 400 years of poetry writing. Remember, none of them were written to fit with each other — the links you make between them are your links.

Other poems feature the theme of bad feelings...
For example, in 'The Farmer's Bride' the bride is filled with terror when faced with her husband.

Section Three — Themes

Negative Emotions

Relationships often involve negative emotions. E.g. "I'm angry — my sister's an idiot" and "I used to like that boy, but I am disgusted by his smelly dog".

> 1) Relationships make us feel a lot of different emotions — not just happy ones.
> 2) Negative emotions include things like jealousy, anger and guilt.

People can be very Bitter

In Paris With You (Pages 22-23)

1) The narrator is very bitter about the end of his previous relationship — "I'm angry at the way I've been bamboozled".
2) He doesn't really seem to give the new relationship much of a chance — "Don't talk to me of love".
3) He often sounds like he feels sorry for himself — "I get tearful".

Sister Maude (Pages 12-13)

1) The narrator is furious with her sister for telling her parents about her lover — "Who told my mother of my shame".
2) She sees her sister as a sneak and a tell-tale — "Who lurked to spy and peer".
3) She wants her sister to suffer for what she did — "Bide *you* with death and sin".

Some people are Jealous or Regretful

Brothers (Pages 28-29)

1) The younger brother seems eager and childlike — "you skipped beside us".
2) But the narrator sounds impatient and frustrated at being "saddled" with him.
3) The narrator wrongly thought he knew it all and felt like an adult — "doing what grown-ups do".
4) Looking back, he knows that he made a bad decision by leaving the youngster behind.
5) He blames himself for the fact that they're not close any more — "the distance I'd set in motion".

The Farmer's Bride (Pages 8-9)

1) The farmer feels uncomfortable about his desire for his young bride who doesn't want him.
2) It seems like he's jealous of the animals his wife talks to — "*I've* hardly heard her speak at all".
3) He shouts out "Oh! my God!" and gets carried away with "the brown, / The brown of her – her eyes, her hair, her hair!".
4) This suggests he's struggling to control his desire.

Other poems feature negative emotions...

'Nettles', 'The Manhunt' and 'Harmonium' are all sad or angry poems — focusing on the fact that relationships, even good ones, may contain some unhappiness.

Section Three — Themes

Love

Relationships aren't just about love — but it is a big part of them. However, you and I have a working relationship, so any feelings you may have for me would be completely inappropriate.

> 1) A lot of poetry is written about love.
> 2) Love for family members and for lovers can be complicated.

Some poems are about Romantic Love

The Manhunt (Pages 18-19)

1) The injured soldier has a <u>loving relationship</u> with his wife, who <u>isn't put off</u> by his wounds.
2) The poet refers to their relationship as "passionate" and "intimate" in the <u>first stanza</u>. This tells the reader how <u>important</u> the physical side of their relationship is.
3) The narrator tries to <u>understand</u> the <u>physical</u> and <u>emotional damage</u> that has been done to him — when she widens "the search" to the "unexploded mine / buried deep in his mind".

Hour (Pages 20-21)

1) Duffy uses <u>personification</u> to explore the different sides of love — "Love's time's beggar".
2) She uses images of <u>precious things</u> to show how much she values love — "treasure", "gold", "jewel".
3) At the end she celebrates how <u>wonderful</u> love is, using <u>repetition</u> to emphasise this — "love spins gold, gold, gold from straw".

"We both love looking at saucy postcards."

Ghazal (Pages 26-27)

1) Her love is so <u>intense</u> it sometimes seems <u>painful</u> — "when the arrow flies, the heart is pierced".
2) At other times, imagery of nature is used to show the <u>pleasure</u> in love — "I am the grass and you the breeze, blow through me".

Some poems are about the love of Parents for their Children

Praise Song For My Mother (Pages 30-31)

1) The narrator talks about <u>how much</u> her mum <u>meant</u> to her — "You were / water to me".
2) She uses the Praise Song to <u>celebrate</u> her mother's <u>love</u> — and say <u>thank you</u> for it.
3) Having given her a <u>great childhood</u>, her mum <u>sent her off</u> to explore the world, without wanting her to feel <u>guilty</u> for leaving — "Go to your wide futures, you said".

Nettles (Pages 14-15)

1) The narrator <u>feels his son's pain</u> ("White blisters beaded") and wants to <u>heal</u> it ("We soothed him").
2) He wants to <u>destroy</u> anything that might <u>hurt</u> his son, but realises that he <u>can't</u> — "My son would often feel sharp wounds again".

Other poems feature the theme of love...

You could contrast any of the more romantic poems with 'In Paris With You', 'The Farmer's Bride' or 'Quickdraw' to show that love isn't always nice.

Section Three — Themes

Time

Poets often like to reflect on time. Maybe it's because they've got so much of it to spare...

> 1) Relationships are all about time — spent together, spent apart, spent growing up, and spent growing old.
> 2) Time is often seen as something that threatens love — damaging the loved one and often taking them away.

Time spent Together is seen as Precious

Hour (Pages 20-21)

1) The poet uses images of valuable things to show how important time spent with her lover is — "we are millionaires".
2) She personifies time to make it seem the enemy of love — "Time hates love, wants love poor".
3) The fairy-tale image of straw being spun into gold suggests that love can win over time.

People look back Fondly on time spent with Loved Ones

Praise Song For My Mother (Pages 30-31)

1) The narrator really values the time that her mum gave to her when she was growing up — "You were / sunrise to me".
2) She sees her mother as a nourishing presence — her love was "warm and streaming".
3) Her mother knew when it was time for the narrator to move away and live her own life — "Go to your wide futures, you said".
4) This suggests how good memories can give confidence for the future.

No time for love — too busy clowning.

Some poets think that love can last Forever

Sonnet 43 (Pages 10-11)

1) In this poem the narrator suggests that love can survive even after death.
2) It seems as if this love has influenced and affected her whole life. It might even have changed how she feels about the time before they met — "I love thee with the breath, / Smiles, tears, of all my life!".

Other poems feature the theme of time...

In 'To His Coy Mistress' the narrator tries to get his mistress to be more adventurous by reminding her that time is passing. 'Harmonium' looks at how the passage of time has damaged the harmonium, but also thinks about how it has affected the narrator's dad.

Section Three — Themes

Getting Older

You can't avoid getting older. It's not all bad — just think, one day you'll be old enough to choose your own poems.

> As time passes, we all grow up and get older — it happens to everyone so it's something lots of poets will write about.

Some poems explore the effects of Ageing on a Relationship

Sonnet 116 (Pages 4-5)

1) The poet says that true love doesn't change, even when people get old and lose their "rosy lips and cheeks". He thinks that how we look isn't important.
2) He even says that true love can survive until "the edge of doom" — the very last day at the end of the world.

To His Coy Mistress (Pages 6-7)

1) The narrator makes youth seem like a one-off opportunity that won't last long — "while the youthful hue / Sits on thy skin like morning dew".
2) He says that getting older is like being chewed up by time — "in his slow-chapt power".
3) He says they should fight the ageing process by grabbing at life's pleasures with enthusiasm — "tear our pleasures with rough strife".

People want to Protect Children as they Grow Up

Nettles (Pages 14-15)

1) The father comforts his very young son after he falls into some nettles.
2) He compares life to a battle. He knows that as his son grows up he won't always be able to protect him from pain — "My son would often feel sharp wounds again".

Born Yesterday (Pages 16-17)

1) Larkin wishes a good and happy life for newborn baby Sally.
2) He knows that most people will wish for Sally "the usual stuff / About being beautiful".
3) But he believes what will really help her to be happy is "An average of talents" — so this is what he wishes for Sally.
4) He uses the poem to show his affection for his friend's newborn daughter and his genuine hope for her future.

Other poems feature the theme of getting older...

'Sonnet 43' looks at the narrator, rather than the other person in the relationship, growing older. 'Brothers' describes a painful memory of growing up and failing to take responsibility.

Section Three — Themes

Death

Death haunts many poems about relationships — it comes for us all in the end.

> 1) Death's an important theme because it marks the end of even the best relationships.
> 2) Some poets symbolise the power of their love by arguing that it'll last beyond death.

Death can be Difficult to Face

Harmonium (Pages 32-33)

1) Removing an old organ from the church makes the narrator's dad talk about his own funeral.
2) The narrator feels awkward about this, and can't think of anything to say — he's "starved of breath".
3) The harmonium is old — its keys are "yellowed …fingernails". His father is also old, "with smoker's fingers and dottled thumbs". Linking the organ to his dad makes it seem like the father is also now past his best.

To His Coy Mistress (Pages 6-7)

1) The narrator tries to use the idea of death to frighten his mistress into a sexual relationship with him — "The grave's a fine and private place, / But none, I think, do there embrace".
2) You could argue that he's scared of his own death — "And yonder all before us lie / Deserts of vast eternity".

Some poets write about Love carrying on beyond Death

Sonnet 116 (Pages 4-5)

1) The poet knows that life will eventually end — "Within his bending sickle's compass come".
2) He personifies time and says that all time gives us is "brief hours and weeks".
3) But he believes that true love will survive beyond the grave until the very last day of earth — "even to the edge of doom".

Sonnet 43 (Pages 10-11)

1) Lots of images — e.g. "soul", "Grace" and "Saints" — link the narrator's love to the idea of religion. This suggests that her love may go beyond life on Earth.
2) In the last line of the poem she says that their love will not only survive after death, it will get even stronger — "I shall but love thee better after death".

Other poems feature the theme of betrayal and death...

'Sister Maude' is about the narrator's extreme reaction to the betrayal and death of her lover.

Section Three — Themes

Memory

Memories of past events can inspire a whole range of emotions.

> 1) Painful memories can haunt people in later life.
> 2) Some memories can represent ongoing problems.

Memories can be Unpleasant to face

The Manhunt (Pages 18-19)

1) The soldier has returned from the war but finds it difficult to deal with what he's been through. He's buried things "deep in his mind".
2) He can't think too deeply about what happened to him — "every nerve in his body had tightened and closed".
3) The poem might have a general message about the effects of war on the people who experience it.

He's smiling blankly in the hope you won't notice he's completely forgotten who you are.

Brothers (Pages 28-29)

1) The narrator remembers leaving his brother behind with regret.
2) He still feels guilty about it, even though it happened a long time ago.
3) The memory of this event seems to have been the source of a "distance" in their relationship.

The Farmer's Bride (Pages 8-9)

1) The farmer remembers when, "Three Summers" ago, he chose his young bride.
2) But after they married she changed and "her smile went out".
3) He recalls how she ran away from him and had to be "chased" and how he "fetched her home".
4) The farmer spends most of the poem describing events that happened in the past. In the second to last stanza, he talks about the present day — his memories are still making him feel bad.

Painful Memories never go away

Nettles (Pages 14-15)

1) The poet remembers when his very young son was hurt.
2) He thinks about his anger at the nettles for causing his son to suffer.
3) He tried to punish the nettles by cutting them down — "slashed in fury" — and then burning them on a "funeral pyre".
4) But he remembers how quickly they grew back — "in two weeks". The memory seems to stick with him because it was the first time he realised he couldn't protect his son completely.

Other poems feature the theme of memory...
'Sonnet 43' suggests that a relationship can draw up feelings from the narrator's childhood.
'Praise Song For My Mother' features the narrator's happy memories of her mother.

Section Three — Themes

Nature

Poets often use images of nature to describe their feelings.

> 1) Natural imagery suggests that something is beautiful and unspoilt.
> 2) Nature can also be used to suggest that something is wild or dangerous.

Natural images can be Positive

Ghazal (Pages 26-27)

1) The poem includes imagery of gardens — "grass", "rose", "bark", "leaf". These show that her love is as natural and beautiful as a garden of paradise.
2) She also includes animals — "bird", "serpent", "hawk", "moth" — which present her love as a living, breathing thing.

Praise Song For My Mother (Pages 30-31)

1) The poet uses imagery connected with the essential elements of life — "water", "sunrise".
2) She also uses food from the country where she grew up — "the fish's red gill", "crab's leg", "fried plantain".
3) She sees her mother as a constant giver of life — "replenishing replenishing".
4) She uses the image of the moon pulling the tide to show how she was drawn to her mother's love — "You were / moon's eye to me / pull".

Sometimes images of Nature can be Sinister

My love for you is like a marmot.

The Farmer's Bride (Pages 8-9)

1) The unhappy bride is compared to small animals — "like a hare", "like a mouse", "shy as a leveret".
2) All of these are prey animals, which suggest she's constantly watching out for predators.
3) Like a wild animal, when she felt cornered "she runned away".

Nettles (Pages 14-15)

1) The nettles are a source of pain for the poet's young son — "With sobs and tears".
2) Their power to harm becomes a metaphor for the pains of life — "My son would often feel sharp wounds again".
3) After the father chops down the nettles they soon grow back — "the busy sun and rain / Had called up tall recruits". This could suggest that suffering is part of nature.

There are other poems that refer to nature...

'Sonnet 116' compares life to a voyage on the ocean and love to a star, which are both natural images. In 'To His Coy Mistress' the narrator suggests that he and his mistress act like birds of prey.

Section Three — Themes

Pain and Desire

Relationships rarely go exactly as we want them to.

> 1) Even in close relationships there are arguments and disagreements.
> 2) Before romantic relationships get going there is sometimes a period of frustrated desire.

Characters in poems sometimes feel Hurt

Quickdraw (Pages 24-25)

1) The narrator is so **desperate** for a call from her lover that she is **carrying** two phones around with her — "I wear the two ... / slung from the pockets on my hips".
2) When she gets the call though, it **hurts** her like she has been shot "through the heart".
3) She describes how **painful** love can be. Even the texted kisses of her lover hit her like bullets — "Take this ... / and this ..."

Harmonium (Pages 32-33)

1) The narrator is unhappy when his **dad** makes a **bad joke** about his death.
2) It seems to **hurt** him more to think about his **dad's death** than it bothers his dad.
3) He **doesn't know how** to **answer** his dad's comments — he can only "mouth in reply / some shallow or sorry phrase or word".

Some characters are motivated by Desire

In Paris With You (Pages 22-23)

1) The character feels that he has been **messed around** by his previous lover — "I'm angry at the way I've been bamboozled".
2) But by the end of the poem his **focus** has shifted onto his physical desire for his **new lover** — "I'm in Paris with your eyes, your mouth".

To His Coy Mistress (Pages 6-7)

1) The narrator makes **no attempt** to disguise the fact that he's **motivated** by **physical desire**.
2) He suggests that while his mistress may not have **welcomed** his lust, the chance to enjoy it will soon be **gone**, when he or she **dies** — "And your quaint honour turn to dust, / And into ashes all my lust".
3) He makes his feelings clear by the **effort** that he puts into trying to persuade her, and in the **passionate**, **violent imagery** in the last stanza — "like amorous birds of prey".

Other poems feature pain and desire...

In 'The Farmer's Bride' the farmer is clearly hurt by his wife's rejection of him, and still feels a strong desire for her. 'Hour' has romantic images of both love and physical desire.

Section Three — Themes

Forms of Poetry

I've chosen to write this poem in the form of a revision guide.

> 1) Writing in poetry gives poets freedom from some of the rules of other forms of writing, such as grammar, punctuation and paragraphing.
> 2) But poetic forms often have their own "rules" about structure.

Some Poetic Forms follow a very Strict Pattern

Sonnet 116 (Pages 4-5) and Sonnet 43 (Pages 10-11)

1) The sonnet is a very old poetic form. It's usually used to write about love — that's what Shakespeare and Barrett Browning have done.
2) A sonnet has 14 lines which are written in iambic pentameter. They usually rhyme.
3) Writing to such strict rules keeps the ideas really focused. Every word has to be carefully chosen to fit in with the rhythm and rhyme scheme.

If you're not sure what iambic pentameter is, see the glossary on p.72-73.

Other Forms have Rules about Content

Ghazal (Pages 26-27)

1) The ghazal is a poetic form that is often about the pain of being apart from a loved one.
2) The couplets are supposed to be unconnected, so that each one could be read on its own, or removed without destroying the poem.
3) This poem uses the form to present us with a series of images showing different sides of love.

Some Poems have a much Less Strict Pattern

Quickdraw (Pages 24-25)

1) The uneven structure, with some split lines (enjambment), reflects the poet's uncertainty about what's going to happen.
2) It's as if she can't control the lines of the poem in the same way she can't control the timing and content of the telephone calls.

Harmonium (Pages 32-33)

1) The narrator is remembering a particular time with his dad.
2) He arranges the poem into stanzas which show different moments from the memory.
3) There's not much of a rhythm or rhyme scheme — it's like he's working his way through the memory and exploring the feelings he had at the time.

You could talk about form with any poem...

Some poems play around with form. 'Hour' starts out like a Shakespearean sonnet, discussing time and love in personified terms, but messes around with the form a bit by using different line lengths.

Poetic Devices

Poetic devices are all those little tricks poets use to liven up their writing. The crazy cats.

> 1) You need to be able to identify different techniques used in the poems and make comparisons between them.
> 2) You also need to say what effect they have on the poem.

Strawberry's my favourite flavour of enjambment.

Poetic Devices include Enjambment...

To His Coy Mistress (Pages 6-7)

1) The enjambment makes the narrator's thoughts seem spontaneous — "Thou by the Indian Ganges' side / Shouldst rubies find; I by the tide / Of Humber would complain..."
2) It's as though he's thinking up things on the spot to persuade his mistress.

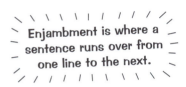

Enjambment is where a sentence runs over from one line to the next.

Hour (Pages 20-21)

1) The poet is recalling a precious hour of love when time seemed to stand still.
2) The enjambment slows the poem down to reflect this — "Time slows, for here / we are millionaires".

...Layout...

Quickdraw (Pages 24-25)

1) The narrator doesn't know when the telephone call will come. When the phone does suddenly ring, the call is painful.
2) Indenting "You've wounded me" and "through the heart" emphasises the pain the character feels.

Praise Song For My Mother (Pages 30-31)

1) The mother's love supports her child emotionally.
2) Offsetting the repeated word "replenishing" sums up the narrator's positive view of her mother.

...and Repetition

The Manhunt (Pages 18-19)

1) The repeated phrase "only then" is important — it emphasises the fact that she's taking small steps and making slow progress.
2) This repetition suggests that it takes time and patience for the narrator to understand her husband's mental state and for him to allow her to see his pain.

You can find poetic devices in most poems...

'Praise Song For My Mother' uses repetition of "You were..." to emphasise the different aspects of her relationship with her mother. 'Brothers' uses enjambment to give it a conversational tone.

Section Four — Poetry Techniques

Beginnings of Poems

The beginning's as good a place to start as any.

> 1) The beginning of any poem is really important as it sets out what the poem is going to be about.
> 2) It can also set the tone for a poem — if it's going to be angry, happy, bitter, etc...

Beginnings can be used to Set the Scene

Nettles (Pages 14-15)

1) The first line gives a straightforward opening. It clearly tells the reader what the poem is going to be about.
2) But from the very next line, the poem begins to explore metaphorical images — looking at the idea of a nettle "bed" and introducing the battle metaphor which is extended throughout the poem — "spears".

Beginnings can also Set the Tone

See the glossary on p.72-73 for explanations of technical terms like 'rhetorical questions' and 'colloquial'.

Sister Maude (Pages 12-13)

1) The first stanza tells us how bitter the narrator is about her sister Maude.
2) She uses rhetorical questions to show that she knows exactly who told her parents about the secret relationship she was having — "Who told my father of my dear?"
3) By the end of the first stanza we're in no doubt about how she sees Maude's actions — "Who lurked to spy and peer".

In Paris With You (Pages 22-23)

1) A sense of hurt and bitterness is shown in the very first sentence — "Don't talk to me of love".
2) The colloquial language ("I've had an earful") is continued in the rest of the poem, giving it an ironic tone.

Born Yesterday (Pages 16-17)

1) The narrator says at the start that his wish for Sally is going to be different from that of other people.
2) The first lines suggest he's going to wish the baby something special — "something / None of the others would".
3) We're surprised when he goes on to wish her not to be too talented or attractive.

You could talk about the beginning of any poem...

'The Manhunt' starts out with what could be the opening lines of a standard love poem — it's only later we realise it's about the effects of war. 'Hour' begins in a fairly similar way to 'Sonnet 116', but then takes on a more intimate tone.

Section Four — Poetry Techniques

Couplets and Last Lines

Writers often try to make their poems go out with a bang.

> 1) The last lines of poems often leave the reader with a powerful image or idea.
> 2) They can also be used to provide a twist — something unexpected.

Closing Couplets and Last Lines can Sum Up a Poem

Sonnet 116 (Pages 4-5)

1) The last two lines of a Shakespearean sonnet rhyme.
2) In this sonnet, the narrator says that everything he's said about love in the poem is true.
3) He says that if it isn't true, then he never wrote anything, and no man has ever been in love.
4) He's challenging the reader to disagree with him — it makes him sound confident that he's right.

Praise Song For My Mother (Pages 30-31)

1) The last line is on its own, making it stand out from the rest of the poem.
2) The last line sums up her mum's generosity in encouraging her child to leave and discover her own destiny.
3) The last lines also suggest a goodbye, and the end of the stage in the narrator's life when she relied on her mum.

"My poem won't have a last line. That'll learn 'em."

Closing Lines can be Surprising

Brothers (Pages 28-29)

1) The poem's last line tells the reader that this isn't just a simple story about a childhood event.
2) When the narrator says he was "unable to close the distance I'd set in motion", he could also be talking about a distance that appeared in his relationship with his younger brother.
3) This gives the poem a sad and reflective ending.

The Farmer's Bride (Pages 8-9)

1) The farmer has told the story of his young bride and how she doesn't like him — "she turned afraid / Of love and me".
2) We know they don't sleep in the same room, "She sleeps up in the attic there / Alone".
3) The final lines are passionate, as he thinks about how attractive she is.
4) There's also a troubling mood to the end of the poem — we get the sense he is struggling to control his desires. The poem finishes with a feeling of threat.

These other poems have interesting endings...

'Nettles' ends with the sad conclusion that painful events will often be repeated and can't be prevented. 'Born Yesterday' uses a final rhyming couplet to give a powerful, heartfelt ending.

Section Four — Poetry Techniques

Rhyme and Rhythm

Rhyme and rhythm are what make poetry poetry.

> 1) Poets can use rhyme to emphasise thoughts and emotions.
> 2) Poets can use rhythm to help fix their words in the reader's memory —
>   just like a catchy tune.

Rhyme can add Force to the poet's message

Ghazal (Pages 26-27)
1) The last but one word of each stanza rhymes — "then woo me ... tattoo me ... bedew me ... pursue me... renew me". It makes the narrator sound urgent and passionate.
2) The repeated rhymes add to a sense of expectation because we want to know how each stanza is going to fit in with the rhyme.

Born Yesterday (Pages 16-17)
1) This poem doesn't have much rhyme, but it ends with a rhyming couplet.
2) This emphasises the contrast between the chatty beginning with its ironic tone, and the sincere message in the final couplet.

The Rhythm can make things Stand Out

Sister Maude (Pages 12-13)
1) The regular rhythm in the first stanza makes the narrator sound angry and hateful — "Who told my mother of my shame".
2) The poem is made up of short words, e.g. "Bide *you* with death and sin". These emphasise the rhythm and keep the poem moving at a fast pace. This also helps give the poem its angry tone.

The Farmer's Bride (Pages 8-9)
1) This poem has a regular rhythm when the farmer is calmly describing events.
2) But sometimes the rhythm changes — this happens when strong emotions are present.
3) In the second stanza, we learn about the bride's escape and recapture. The rhythm here gets faster, a bit like her frightened run across the fields — "We chased her, flying like a hare".

These other poems use rhyme and rhythm...
'Quickdraw' uses internal rhymes, which emphasise its unpredictable structure.
'In Paris With You' uses funny and unexpected rhymes to give it a slightly ironic tone.

Section Four — Poetry Techniques

Use of First Person

Writing in the first person can be a good way of expressing personal feelings.
I like writing in the first person.

> 1) A poem written in the first person is one where the narrator is a character in the poem — it'll use words like "I" and "me".
> 2) Other poems are written in the third person — e.g. "She rode her bicycle".
> 3) Writing in the first person gives the poet a chance to describe the world from their own or a character's point of view.

Writing in the First Person can express Personal Feelings

The Manhunt (Pages 18-19)

1) The wife of the injured soldier *explores* her husband's injuries.
2) The use of the *first person* means we go through the process with her — "only then could I picture the scan".
3) The first person narrator sounds *calm*. This makes the poem sound calm, even though it's about a *tense*, painful subject.

Hour (Pages 20-21)

1) The narrator uses *first person* to show how happy love makes her — "we kiss".
2) Using the *first person* makes the reader feel like they're *sharing* the experience with her, not just *witnessing* it.
3) The poem starts in the *third person*, talking about love and time in general. This makes the part where the narrator starts talking about her *own experience* of love stand out — "We find an hour together...".

It can add Impact to the Poem

Brothers (Pages 28-29)

1) The *guilt* that the narrator feels at having run off and left his six-year-old brother is *shared* with the reader.
2) He reveals his feelings of *frustration* directly — "I sighed".

He'd quit poetry to concentrate on becoming the first person.

In Paris With You (Pages 22-23)

1) The narrator continually talks about *himself* — "I've had an earful", "I get tearful", "I'm one of your...", "I'm angry".
2) This shows how *self-absorbed* he is — "I'm a hostage. I'm marooned".
3) Putting the poem in the *first person* means that it's as if we're the ones being spoken to. Rather than just being a story, we're made to *feel* as if *we are there*.

Other poems are in the first person...

Putting the narrative in first person gives 'The Farmer's Bride' an added tension because we get a look at the farmer's state of mind as well as a description of the events.

Section Four — Poetry Techniques

Imagery

Imagery is language that creates a picture in your mind.

> 1) Imagery helps the reader imagine the people, places and feelings in a poem.
> 2) Imagery includes things like metaphors and similes.
> Look these up the glossary on p.72-73 if you're not sure what they are.

"We'd like more poems with fishing imagery."

Some poets translate Time into Imagery

Sonnet 116 (Pages 4-5)

1) Shakespeare personifies time as an old man with a "sickle" for harvesting corn. This is a traditional image which links time with death.
2) When Shakespeare says that love can outsmart time — "Love's not Time's fool" — he's suggesting it can also beat death.

If you personify something, you write about it like it's a person with thoughts and feelings.

Poets use a lot of Natural Imagery

Ghazal (Pages 26-27)

1) This poem compares the narrator and her lover to plants and animals.
2) The poet uses these images to play with ideas of power in the relationship. Sometimes she makes herself seem weak — "I am the laurel leaf in your crown" — and sometimes dangerous — "If mine is the venomous tongue, the serpent's tail".
3) The natural images also show that there's a darker side to love. The phrase "hawk to my shadow" suggests an animal-like attraction, but also a dangerous one.

Nettles (Pages 14-15)

1) The poet personifies the bed of nettles as an army. He carries on this metaphor when he compares the accident to an act of war — "spears", "recruits".
2) This helps the poet show the importance of an everyday event.

Praise Song For My Mother (Pages 30-31)

1) The mum in this poem gave her children everything they needed when they were little. To show this, the poet uses lots of natural images, e.g. "water", "sunrise", "moon" and images of food.
2) The choice of food imagery also ties the poem in to a particular place and time.
3) The overall effect is to show that the mum was the centre of the narrator's world.

There's plenty of imagery in these poems...

'To His Coy Mistress' also uses imagery connected with time, but for very different reasons than 'Sonnet 116'. 'The Farmer's Bride' uses a lot of natural imagery to describe the bride.

Section Four — Poetry Techniques

Unusual Vocabulary

This page is all about the weird and wacky words of poets. Ka-boom.

> Sometimes poets will use language in unusual ways to get the reader to notice something.

Strange Words force the reader to take Another Look

Quickdraw (Pages 24-25)

1) The repetition of the final words "Take this" continues the theme of a gunfight in an old Western film or TV show.
2) These words are like bullets fired out of a gun — this sums up the connection between modern communications and the Wild West imagery in the poem.

Harmonium (Pages 32-33)

1) The poet uses alliteration to describe the music of the harmonium, "its hummed harmonics... for a hundred years".
2) The third stanza of the poem is about the harmony between generations of fathers and sons as they sang in the choir — "had opened their throats / and gilded finches... had streamed out".
3) This strange image stands out against the mostly normal, down-to-earth language of the rest of the poem.

Vocabulary can help describe Characters

The Farmer's Bride (Pages 8-9)

1) The farmer speaks in his own dialect — "'twasn't a woman", "Tis but a stair / Betwixt us".
2) This makes him sound like a real person — and because of this we feel a bit sorry for him. We realise he probably didn't mean to scare his young bride.

Praise Song For My Mother (Pages 30-31)

1) The poet chooses her words carefully. This makes her descriptions of her mum short, but very effective, e.g. "You were / sunrise to me".
2) Some of her words don't have a simple meaning — "fathoming" suggests both a great depth and great understanding and "mantling" suggests covering and protecting.
3) This helps show how complex her mother's love was.

You can find unusual vocabulary in other poems too...

'To His Coy Mistress' contains such odd turns of phrase as "vegetable love". When you notice something odd in these poems, have a good think about why the poet might have used those words.

Section Four — Poetry Techniques

Irony and Sarcasm

Why can't they just say what they mean?

> 1) Irony is when you say one thing and mean another. It's often used in a funny way, but can also have a more serious meaning.
> 2) Sarcasm is like irony, but has a cruel twist to it.

Irony can express Painful Memories

Nettles (Pages 14-15)

1) The poet thinks that the term "nettle bed" is ironic.
2) He calls it a "curious name", because "It was no place for rest".
3) A child's bed should be safe and comfortable — but the nettles hurt the little boy, so it seems strange to call the clump of nettles a bed.

Brothers (Pages 28-29)

1) In the poem, the big brothers think they're grown-up — but looking back, the narrator knows they weren't.
2) The two elder brothers think they're mature, but ironically this just makes it clear that they're children — "I was nine and he was ten / and we must stroll the town, doing what grown-ups do".

Poets use Sarcasm to Make a Point

To His Coy Mistress (Pages 6-7)

1) The narrator exaggerates how much time he'd like to spend flirting with his mistress — "An hundred years should go to praise / Thine eyes".
2) This exaggeration is called hyperbole. He's sarcastically making fun of traditional ideas about love. He sees the delay as a waste of time.
3) He also uses sarcasm to frighten his mistress with the thought of death — "The grave's a fine and private place, / But none, I think, do there embrace".

See the glossary on p.72-73 for explanations of technical terms like 'hyperbole'.

Born Yesterday (Pages 16-17)

1) Larkin writes ironically about "the usual stuff" which people wish for a baby, e.g. "running off a spring / Of innocence and love".
2) He doubts that it's possible to live up to this ideal — "Well, you're a lucky girl". His sarcasm makes these ideals seem unrealistic.

These poems also contain irony and sarcasm...

'In Paris With You' is set in the romantic city of Paris, but a lot of the descriptions aren't romantic at all. It also mixes the narrator's misery with humorous rhymes.

Section Four — Poetry Techniques

Mood

Mood is the general feel and emotion of the poem. Not what the cow did.

> 1) Poets create a mood with their choice of words and descriptions.
> 2) The situation and events of the poem also contribute to the mood.

"Poems always put me in a mood".

Some poets create an Unhappy Mood

The Farmer's Bride (Pages 8-9)

1) At the end of this poem, we're left with a winter scene — "the black earth spread white with rime". Winter is often used to show unhappiness in poetry.
2) This contrasts with the spring imagery the narrator uses to describe his wife — "Sweet as the first wild violets". Spring suggests new life and hope — but by the end of the poem, that's all in the past.

Harmonium (Pages 32-33)

1) The mood in this poem is quite sad. This is created through the image of the old harmonium, which is no longer being used by the church.
2) The narrator also thinks a lot about what might have happened to the organ in the past — "holes were worn in both the treadles / where the organist's feet... had pedalled". This gives the poem a reflective mood.
3) The poem ends with a serious mood. This is the result of the dad's joke about death in the final stanza.

Mood can be shown in Different Ways

In Paris With You (Pages 22-23)

1) The writer is clearly upset about his last relationship — "Don't talk to me of love... I get tearful". So there is a bitter note in the poem's mood.
2) The mood is made complex by the setting — we expect it to be romantic because it's Paris, but it's described in a really unromantic way — "sleazy hotel".

Sonnet 43 (Pages 10-11)

1) The poet uses repetition and religious language to build up a passionate mood — "I love thee purely".
2) The poet uses an outburst of short words to describe how her love is part of her whole life — "I love thee with the breath, / Smiles, tears, of all my life!" This gives the poem a more emotional and less controlled mood.

Think about the mood of all these poems...

'To His Coy Mistress' is both passionate and witty. 'Sister Maude' uses alliteration and repetition to convey a very angry mood. The loose form of 'Hour' gives it quite a relaxed, romantic mood.

Section Four — Poetry Techniques

SECTION FIVE — THE POETRY EXAM

The Poetry Exam: Unit Two Overview

If you're following Route A of the AQA English Literature course, you'll have to do an exam called Unit 2: Poetry Across Time. That's what this page is all about.

Your Exam Will be Split Up Like This

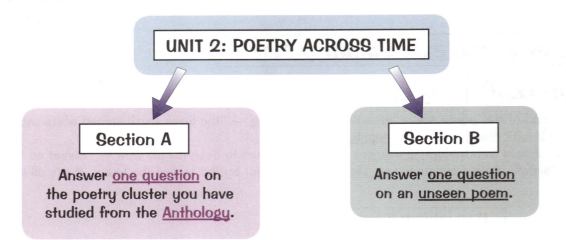

1) This guide contains all the poems from the 'Relationships' cluster of the Anthology — this should be the one you've studied in class. There are three other poetry clusters, which you don't need to worry about.
2) The next few pages will give you tips on how to answer the question in Section A.
3) Section A is worth two-thirds of the marks in the exam and nearly a quarter of your entire GCSE.

This is How Your Exam Will Work

1) The whole exam lasts 1 hour 15 minutes. You should spend about 45 minutes on Section A. The other 30 minutes should be spent doing Section B.
2) Section A has a choice of two questions for each poetry cluster. You should only answer one question and it should be about the cluster you've studied. The question is worth 36 marks.
3) You're not allowed to take your own anthology or any notes about the poems into the exam. You'll be given a blank copy of the anthology to help you with your answer.
4) You'll also be given a separate answer book to write your answer in.

There are Instructions on the Front Page of the Exam

1) You must read the front page of the exam paper before you start — it tells you exactly what to do.
2) There will be a list of things you need for the exam. Make sure you've got everything on it.
3) Check you've got the right exam paper — it should be the one for foundation tier.
4) Remember to fill in all the details on the front page of the answer booklet.

I hope you're paying attention — there's an exam on this...

I like pages like this. Absolutely no learning whatsoever. Lovely. Don't worry if you forget some of this stuff — there'll be a reminder of how the exam works on the front page of the exam paper.

Section Five — The Poetry Exam

Sample Question 1

OK, so now you know what the exam's about. I bet you're just dying to find out what the questions will be like, eh? Er, well... Here's your first sample question anyway.

Read the Question Carefully and Underline Key Words

1) You'll have a choice of two questions, so it's best to read them both through carefully first. Then pick the one you think you've got the best chance of answering well.
2) Once you've done that, read the question you've chosen through again. Underline the question's theme and any other important words.
3) The question will give you the title of one poem and ask you to compare it to one other poem of your choice. Pick another poem you think relates to the theme.
4) Look up the poems you're going to write about in the blank copy of the anthology you'll be given in the exam. Turn over the corners of the pages they're on so you can find them again quickly.

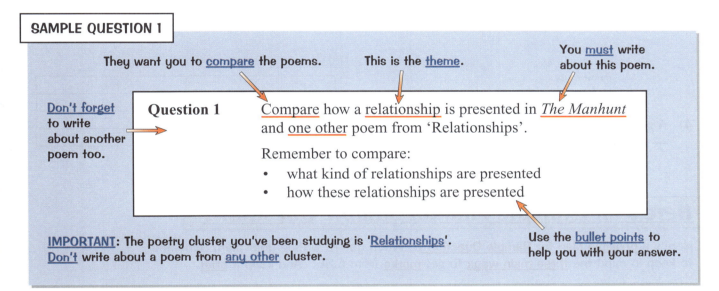

SAMPLE QUESTION 1

They want you to compare the poems. | This is the theme. | You must write about this poem.

Don't forget to write about another poem too.

Question 1 Compare how a relationship is presented in *The Manhunt* and one other poem from 'Relationships'.

Remember to compare:
• what kind of relationships are presented
• how these relationships are presented

IMPORTANT: The poetry cluster you've been studying is 'Relationships'. Don't write about a poem from any other cluster.

Use the bullet points to help you with your answer.

There are Three Main Ways to Get Marks

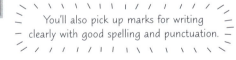
You'll also pick up marks for writing clearly with good spelling and punctuation.

Whichever question you choose to answer, you'll get marks for:

1) Giving your own thoughts and opinions on the poems and supporting them with quotes from the text.
2) Explaining features like form, structure and language.
3) Describing the similarities and differences between poems.

In 18th century Scotland, the penalty for forgetting to include quotes was severe.

Keep these three things in mind when you're writing and planning your answer.

Read the question carefully...

If only I'd always followed that particular piece of advice myself — there might never have been that unfortunate incident with the policeman and the chocolate orange. Still, we live and learn.

Section Five — The Poetry Exam

Planning

If you were to ask me what my best tip would be for getting great marks in your exam, I would not say "bribe the examiner". Oh no. That would be wrong. I'd say "plan your essay answer".

Spend Five Minutes Planning Your Answer

1) Always plan your answer before you start — that way, you're less likely to forget something important.
2) Write your plan at the top of your answer booklet and draw a neat line through it when you've finished.
3) Don't spend too long on your plan. It's only rough work, so you don't need to write in full sentences. Here are a few examples of different ways you can plan your answer:

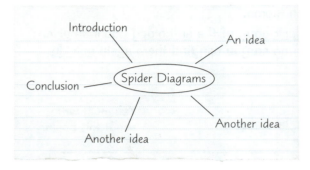

Bullet points with...
- Intro...
- An idea...
- The next idea...

Tables with...

A point...	Quote to back this up...
Another point...	Quote...
A different point...	Quote...
A brand new point...	Quote...

4) A good plan will help you organise your ideas — and write a good, well-structured essay.

Here's an Example Plan for Sample Question 1

Here's a possible plan for Sample Question 1. When you're writing your plan, remember to keep in mind the three main ways to get marks from p.55. And keep it brief.

Plan: poem 1 = The Manhunt, poem 2 = Nettles
1) Introduction — kind of relationships in each poem
- Poem 1 — wife — passion, love, care for husband
- Poem 2 — love and care too

2) Language Comparison
- Poem 1 — soldier seems delicate — 'porcelain', 'parachute silk' show he's fragile
- Poem 2 — again, war imagery — dad's need to protect son

3) Form and Structure Comparison
- Poem 1 — rhyming couplets — simple rhyme contrasts with serious subject
- Poem 2 — simple rhyme scheme, serious subject

4) Message of poems — why poem was written
- Poem 1 — describes wife's feelings for husband / effects of war on individuals
- Poem 2 — describes parent's feelings for child

5) Summary — Comparing — 'Both these poems...'

Use your plan to start making links between the poems.

Jot down any good quotes you want to use.

Don't forget to write about language, form and structure.

Write about ideas and attitudes too.

You can't write a great essay without a good plan...

This is time well spent — five minutes spent planning your answer in an exam will help you get a much better mark. Practise by planning your own answers to the sample questions in this guide.

Section Five — The Poetry Exam

**THIS IS A FLAP.
FOLD THIS PAGE OUT.**

Mark Scheme

If I were you, I'd be <u>pretty keen</u> to find out what the <u>examiner</u> expected of me right about now. Oh yes, it'd definitely feature somewhere in my <u>top 20</u> things to do when bored. Maybe top 50.

Look at <u>What You Have to Do</u> to Get Each <u>Grade</u>

Here are the <u>kind of things</u> you'll need to do to get <u>different grades</u>.
You'll need to match <u>most or all</u> of these to get the grade they describe.

Grade	What you've written
C	<ul><li>Comments clearly on several aspects of the poems, e.g. mood, language, feelings, and uses quotes to back the comments up</li><li>Makes plenty of comparisons between the poems</li><li>Explains <u>how</u> language, form and structure affect the reader</li><li>Makes valid comments about themes, attitudes or feelings in the poems</li></ul>
D	<ul><li>Comments clearly on the poems and uses quotes to back up several points</li><li>Makes several comparisons between the poems</li><li>Identifies the effects of language, form and structure on the reader</li><li>Talks about some of the themes, attitudes or feelings in the poems</li></ul>
E	<ul><li>Comments on the poems and uses occasional quotes to back up some points</li><li>Makes occasional comparisons between the poems</li><li>Shows some understanding of language, form or structure</li><li>Gives a rough overview of the themes, attitudes or feelings in the poems</li></ul>
F	<ul><li>Makes some comments about the poems, mentioning some details from the text</li><li>Occasionally makes simple links between the poems</li><li>Shows a basic understanding of language, form or structure</li><li>Mentions some of the themes, attitudes or feelings in the poems</li></ul>
G	<ul><li>Makes a simple comment (or comments) about the poems</li><li>May suggest a link between the poems</li><li>Mentions something about language, form or structure</li><li>Mentions one of the themes, attitudes or feelings in the poems</li></ul>

> You'll also be marked on your <u>spelling</u>, <u>punctuation</u> and <u>grammar</u>.
> To get the most marks your work should be <u>clear</u> and <u>easy to understand</u>.

Section Five — The Poetry Exam

Sample Question 2

Okey doke, here's another Sample Question for you — it's number two of three, you lucky thing. Have a think about how you'd answer it, then turn over for an example of how you could do it.

Here's Sample Question 2

This is another example of the type of question that might come up in your exam. Remember to read the question carefully and underline key words.

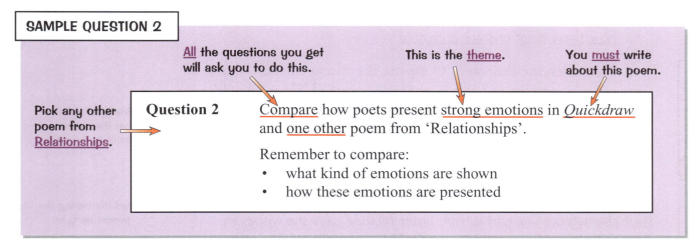

Here's an Example Plan for Sample Question 2

Here's an example of a different way you could plan your answer. Remember, you need to start thinking up comparisons between the poems at the planning stage.

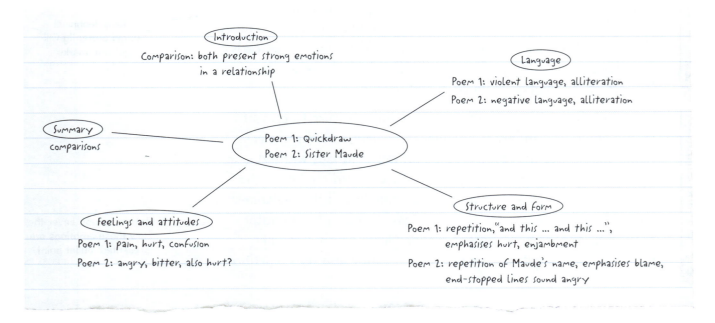

Try out different types of plans to see what's best for you...

When you're writing answers to practice exam questions, try doing your plan a bit differently each time — that way, you can work out the best way to organise your ideas before the real thing.

Section Five — The Poetry Exam

How to Answer the Question

Here's a 'C' grade sample answer to the exam question on p.59.

> Compare how poets present strong emotions in 'Quickdraw'
> and one other poem from 'Relationships'.
>
> Remember to compare:
> - what kind of emotions are shown
> - how these emotions are presented

1 Introduction

Poets often use their work to explore the strong emotions that surround relationships and this is what the writers of 'Sister Maude' and 'Quickdraw' have done. In 'Sister Maude', the narrator is angry with her sister for telling their parents about a secret love affair she had, while the narrator of 'Quickdraw' is hurt by her lover's text messages and phone calls.

Briefly summarise what the poems are about in the intro.

2 Language

Both poets use negative language to express the feelings of their characters. The narrator in 'Sister Maude' says she wishes her sister "no sleep / Either early or late". This suggests she is so angry with Maude that she wants her to suffer even after she is dead. This is a very strong reaction to her crime. The poem 'Quickdraw' also uses violent imagery to show the narrator's pain. The speaker uses words to do with weapons and conflict to describe how her lover's words affect her: "your voice a pellet". The two characters appear to be part of a Wild West gunfight that the narrator is losing: "I reel. / Down on my knees". Both poets use alliteration to stress the emotions in their poems. For example, in 'Sister Maude', the phrase "Cold he lies, as cold as stone, / With his clotted curls" sounds upset and angry. Similarly, in 'Quickdraw', the words "trigger of my tongue" seem cruel and unkind.

Start comparing the poems early on.

Use short quotes to back up your points.

Using technical terms correctly will get you marks.

3 Form and Structure

Both Rossetti and Duffy use form and structure to present strong emotions. In 'Sister Maude', the repetition of her sister's name emphasises the fact that the narrator is furious with Maude. By repeating the word "sister", the reader can also see how bitter she is. This is because the two girls are family and their relationship should be a happy and loving one. Rossetti makes her narrator seem even angrier by using end-stopped lines, which make her sound like she is spitting out her words. Duffy also uses repetition

Make sure you cover the 'how these emotions are presented' bullet point.

Section Five — The Poetry Exam

How to Answer the Question

to show her narrator's pain in 'Quickdraw'. In the final line, the lover's kisses are like bullets shot from a gun: "Take this ... / and this ... and this ... and this ...". Unlike Rossetti, Duffy uses enjambment. The lines are split irregularly to add to the poem's tension. Some of the split lines are indented, which adds emphasis to their words, for example, "You've wounded me" and "through the heart".

Keep using quotes to support your ideas.

In both poems, the narrator is shown as the victim. Each speaker has been hurt by a loved one, but they react to this pain in very different ways. Rossetti's narrator is angry and wants to cut all ties with her sister. The narrator of 'Quickdraw', on the other hand, is still desperate to hear from her lover. Even though the relationship hurts her, she doesn't want it to end. Both these poems also show that relationships can sometimes have an unpleasant side. The narrator of 'Sister Maude' appears to really hate her sister. This is probably because she trusted her and was shocked by her betrayal. 'Quickdraw' shows that romantic relationships are not always about love and tenderness either. Here, the two lovers are each trying to cause the other person the most pain.

Talk about differences as well as similarities.

Stay focused on the theme of 'strong emotions'.

Feelings and Attitudes — 4

The narrator's strong emotions are clearly presented in both 'Sister Maude' and 'Quickdraw'. Although the form of the two poems is quite different, Rossetti and Duffy both use negative and sometimes violent language to show their characters' feelings. The narrators of both poems have been hurt by someone they love and trust. In 'Sister Maude', this pain has turned into anger. In 'Quickdraw', it has led to unhappiness and confusion. Many of us will have experienced similar emotions in our own relationships at one time or another, so we can easily understand the suffering of both individuals.

Use the conclusion to sum up your ideas.

Conclusion — 5

Section Five — The Poetry Exam

Sample Question 3

Most of the questions you get in the exam will be pretty similar. One or two might look a bit different, but they shouldn't cause you any major problems — just follow the advice on this page.

Here's Sample Question 3

Some questions are worded a bit differently — don't let them catch you out. Here's an example:

SAMPLE QUESTION 3

Be careful with this question — it isn't asking you for a rant about how much you hate these poems. The mark scheme is the same as for the other questions — you still need to comment on language, form and structure.

Question 3	Different people prefer different poems. Write about whether you enjoyed the poem *The Farmer's Bride* and compare it to one other poem from 'Relationships' which you either like or dislike.

Remember to compare:
- the relationships and other ideas in the poems
- how each poem has been written

You're still being asked to compare the two poems.

It's not enough just to say which bits you like or dislike.

Here's an Example Plan for Sample Question 3

Here's another way you could plan your answer. The table helps you sort out which quotes you want to use to support each of the points you make.

Intro
Poem 1: The Farmer's Bride, Poem 2: Harmonium
Response: both poems describe characters in difficult situations

	Poem 1	Poem 2
Form: both narrative poems	rhyming couplets: "swift as he / ... young larch tree"	free verse, occasional rhyme for emphasis, "freight", "weight"
Different types of lang: Poem 1 — personification Poem 2 — nature, hunting	"Frightened fay", "Shy as a leveret", "like a mouse", "We chased her"	"hummed harmonics", "yellowed... fingernails", "lost its tongue"
Wider Issues: both create sympathy for characters	"I've hardly heard her speak at all"	"some shallow or sorry phrase or word"

Preference
FB — uses effective metaphors
Harmonium most effective — emotional last line, realism

Always write about language, form and structure...

Don't panic if something a bit odd like this comes up in the exam. It's really asking you to do the same as you would in any other question — so just write your answer in the same way.

Section Five — The Poetry Exam

THIS IS A FLAP.
FOLD THIS PAGE OUT.

SECTION SIX — CONTROLLED ASSESSMENT

The Controlled Assessment

If you're following Route B of the AQA English Literature course, you'll have to do a controlled assessment task for Unit 5: Exploring Poetry. That's what this page is about.

This is How Unit 5 Works

1) Your teacher will set you a question on some poetry. They might decide to use poems from the poetry Anthology that's covered in this book.
2) The question will ask you to compare contemporary poems (like those in Section 2) with ones from the Literary Heritage (Section 1).
3) You might have to listen to or watch performances of the poems and write about them in your answer.
4) You're expected to write around 2000 words. Your answer is worth 25% of your final GCSE grade.

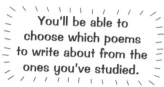

You'll be able to choose which poems to write about from the ones you've studied.

You're Allowed to Plan Your Answer First

1) You'll be able to spend time in class planning and preparing your answer.
2) During this time, you'll be allowed to look at books and the Internet and ask your teacher questions. You must make a note of anything you use to help you (e.g. a website) in a bibliography.
3) You can write a rough draft if you want, but you won't be able to have it with you while you're writing up your answer. You can take in brief notes though.

You'll Have Four Hours to Write Up Your Answer

1) You can write up your answer in your classroom over a few lessons, but you'll be under exam conditions.

2) You'll be given unmarked copies of the poems to help you.

3) You can write up your essay by hand, or type it up on a computer.

> You'll be allowed a dictionary or to use your spell-check, but if you do have a computer you won't be able to get on the Internet.

4) Your work will be collected in at the end of every session. When you've finished, your teacher will collect in everything you've written — including any drafts you did earlier on.

For Sam's control assessment he had to demonstrate skilful changing of channels.

You'll write up the task under exam conditions...

So, your teacher will set you a question on some poems you've studied. You'll have time to prepare your answer, but you're expected to write it up in a maximum of four supervised hours.

Section Six — Controlled Assessment

The Controlled Assessment

I expect you'd find it helpful to know what kind of questions you're going to get asked, how best to approach them and what you'll be marked on. So I've done a nice page about it for you.

You'll Be Marked on Three Main Things

Whatever question you get, you'll get marks for doing these three things.

Keep them in mind when you're planning and writing your answer.

1. Giving your own thoughts and opinions on the poems and supporting the points you make with quotes from the text.
2. Explaining features like form, structure and language.
3. Describing the similarities and differences between poems.

This means you should always compare the poems you're writing about.

Here Are Some Example Questions

EXAMPLE QUESTION 1

Explore the ways different types of relationships are presented in the texts you have studied.

EXAMPLE QUESTION 2

Explore how poets use structure and form to create an effect in a range of contemporary and Literary Heritage poems.

1) You can choose which poems you write about, but you must include at least one contemporary and one Literary Heritage poem. The number of poems you write about is up to you, but make sure you have plenty to say about each one.
2) You have to compare the poems throughout your answer to get good marks.

Think About How You're Going to Tackle the Question

The question you get will be quite general, so you're going to have to think about the best way to approach it. You might find it helpful to start off with a basic plan covering the things below.

- Choose poems which relate to the theme of the question.
- Look at the language — what effect does it create? How does it do this?
- Look at the form and structure — what effect do they create? How do they do this?
- What are the feelings and attitudes in the poems?

} How do the poems compare with each other?

Prepare your answer carefully...

The question you get will be pretty general, but you'll always be marked in the same way. Always write about language, form and structure, as well as the feelings and attitudes in the poems.

Section Six — Controlled Assessment

The Controlled Assessment

A good plan will help you organise your thoughts and write a clear, well-structured essay — which means lots of lovely marks. And the good news is, you'll have plenty of time to prepare one.

Choose Your Poems and Map Out Ideas

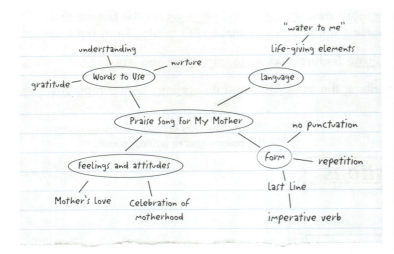

1) Let's say that for Example Question 1 on page 65, you decide to write about 'Praise Song For My Mother'.

2) You might want to map out your ideas like I have on the left, so you can decide what to include in your detailed plan.

3) It's a good idea to do this for all the poems you've chosen to write about. Try to make links between them.

4) Write down some key quotes you want to include in your essay too.

Write a Detailed Plan

Here's an example plan for Question 1 on the last page. You can make it fairly detailed, as you've got enough time.

For some ideas on different ways to plan, see page 56.

Introduction
What essay is about
Negative poems: Sister Maude, In Paris With You
Positive poems: Praise Song For My Mother, The Manhunt

Feelings and Attitudes
- Sister Maude — anger with sister
- In Paris — bitter about failed relationship
- Praise Song — celebration of mother's love
- The Manhunt — wife's protective love towards injured husband

Language
- Sister Maude — emotive — "lurked"
- In Paris — emotive — "wounded"
- Praise Song — life-giving elements (sun, water, food)
- The Manhunt — link between physical injuries + mental state — "mine" / "mind" half rhyme

Form and Structure
- Sister Maude — short lines, alternating rhyme = sounds angry
- In Paris — half rhymes = funny
- Praise Song — rhythm changes, no punctuation, final line
- The Manhunt — rhyming couplets — cheerful rhyme scheme contrasts with serious subject

Conclusion
- Praise Song and Manhunt show positive relationships, Sister Maude and In Paris present bitter feelings

Plan what you're going to write about before you start...

Use your preparation time wisely to come up with a good plan for your essay. You won't be allowed it with you when you're writing up, but you can have a few notes to jog your memory.

Section Six — Controlled Assessment

The Controlled Assessment

Here are some grade 'C' paragraphs from a sample answer to Example Question 1 on page 65.

Here's a Sample Introduction

Write an introduction that makes it clear you've understood the question, like this one:

> Poems are often written about relationships and the various emotions that surround them. Many relationships are positive and involve emotions such as love and loyalty. Poems which present such relationships include 'Praise Song For My Mother' and 'The Manhunt'. In contrast, some relationships involve negative feelings like anger and bitterness. These less pleasant emotions are dealt with in 'Sister Maude' and 'In Paris With You'.

Tell the reader the names of the poems you're going to discuss.

Here are Some Sample Paragraphs

You've got 2000 words, so try to write about the poems in detail. Remember to back up your argument with quotes too — that's dead important.

> Both 'Sister Maude' and 'In Paris With You' are narrated by people who are angry at being betrayed by a loved one. In 'Sister Maude', the narrator blames Maude for telling their parents about a secret relationship she was in: "Who told my father of my dear? / Oh who but Maude". She repeats Maude's name several times to emphasise the fact that she blames her sister for her lover's death. Repetition of the word "sister" confirms her bitterness and hatred. It reminds us that sisters usually love and support each other, making Maude's crime even greater. The writer of 'In Paris With You' also uses repetition to emphasise...

Make it clear what each paragraph's about in the first line.

Use quotes from the poems.

Remember to compare the poems.

It's important to give your own opinions on the poems. You should also try to say why you think the poem was written or what its message might be.

> 'The Manhunt' uses the relationship between husband and wife to make the reader think about the effects of war on the people involved. The couple are clearly in love, but the husband's injuries make it difficult for the wife to "come close" to him. Short stanzas and repetition of the words "only then", show that the husband's recovery is a slow, step-by-step process. His injuries are very serious and make the reader think carefully about how war affects the people who fight in it. Armitage seems to want us to consider the effect conflict has on real people and their partners or families.

Keep focused on the theme of the question.

Look at the poem's wider messages.

Give your own personal interpretations.

Section Six — Controlled Assessment

SECTION SEVEN — WRITING SKILLS

Making Comparisons

This is the stuff you'll really need to know — how to compare two poems.

Comparing Means Finding Similarities and Differences

1) Comparing means looking at two or more things together.
2) You need to make links between the two poems. Don't just write about one poem then the other.
3) Explain how the two poems are similar and different.
4) Give examples and quotes to back up your ideas.

Different children, same terrible hat.

Questions Use Key Words to Help You

One of the questions in the exam could ask you to compare the way relationships are presented in two poems. The question might look a bit like this:

> 1 Compare the ways that relationships are presented in *Brothers* and one other poem from 'Relationships'.
>
> Remember to compare:
> - the relationships in the poems
> - how the relationships are presented

Write about similarities AND differences.

Talk about how the poets show us the relationships.

Choose a poem that goes well with 'Brothers'.

When you've read the question, you need to work out how to answer it:

1) Choose another poem that links well with the one in the question.
2) Link the poems together by describing their similarities and differences.
3) You can compare feelings, structure, language and ideas.
4) Make a plan showing how you want to compare the poems (see p.56).

Try to Compare the Texts as you Go Along

Here's part of a sample answer to the question above, comparing 'Brothers' with 'Nettles'.

> 'Brothers' and 'Nettles' are both about family relationships. In 'Brothers' the narrator describes being annoyed about having to look after his little brother as a child. 'Nettles', on the other hand, is about a parent who wants to care for his son and protect him from pain.

This phrase shows that the answer is comparing both poems directly.

This word introduces a similarity.

Look at the next page for more linking words.

Compare the poems by finding links between them...

There's a fair bit to remember when you're comparing poems, but this section should help a bit. Have a look at the next page for some more handy linking words for your comparison essays.

69

Linking Words

Another trick you need to practise is using linking words. These are the lovely helpful words that link different points of your essay together and help you make comparisons.

You Need to Link Different Points Together

1) Don't just jump from one point to the next — structure your essay.
2) Use connectives (linking words) to show when you're comparing.
3) Learn a few connectives for talking about similarities and some for describing the differences between poems.
4) Use words like 'therefore' and 'so' for conclusions.

You gotta link stuff together.

Use These Words for Describing Similarities...

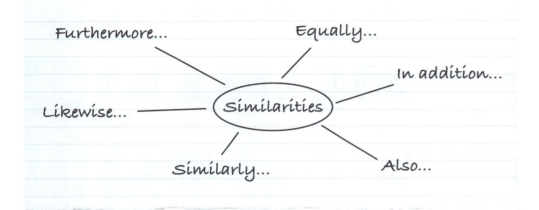

...and These Ones for Differences

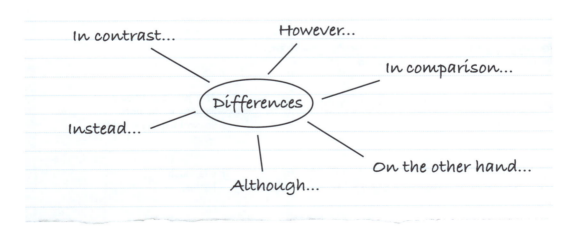

Furthermore, some linking words are also equally similar...

Learn the words on this page and when to use them in your essays. It's a good idea to make it clear to the examiner whether you're talking about similarities or differences between the poems.

Section Seven — Writing Skills

Quoting

Don't just jot down any old stuff — you've got to back it up to get the marks.

You Need to Back Up Your Argument

Writing a good essay is about backing up your points with proper evidence. There are two ways to back up your points:

"One loves to quote."

1) **QUOTING** — Quoting means giving examples from a poem in the exact same words as the original. When you quote something, you have to explain how it backs up your argument.

2) **EXAMPLES** — You can talk about what happens in the poem in your own words. You can make quick points when you haven't got time to quote loads of stuff.

The best way to back up your points is to use direct quotations from the poem. That way you can also talk about the way the poet uses imagery and language.

Always Support Your Ideas with Details from the Text

Here are some quoting top tips:

1) Make sure the quote is relevant.

✓ The narrator says that Maude "lurked to spy and peer". This suggests she was being dishonest.

✗ Barrett Browning says that she will love her husband "to the depth and breadth and height / [Her] soul can reach, when feeling out of sight / For the ends of Being and ideal Grace".
— This bit's not needed.

2) Don't quote large chunks of text — it just wastes time.

3) Don't write long lists of quotes without explaining them.

✗ Mew compares the Farmer's wife to animals: "frightened fay" "like a hare", "like a mouse", "Shy as a leveret".
— This just describes what happens in the poem — it doesn't explain anything.

✓ By comparing the Farmer's wife to a "little, frightened fay", Mew makes her sound vulnerable and scared.
— This is much better.

Make sure you explain what the quote means...

Quotes. Can't live with 'em, can't live without 'em as I believe the saying goes. Or a saying anyway. Think carefully about which ones to use and where, that's my advice. Sorted.

Section Seven — Writing Skills

Structure

You need to know why paragraphs are so important — and also how to write a good one.

Structure Your Answer by Using Paragraphs

You need to organise your points clearly and link them together. The best way to do that is to write in paragraphs. Use a paragraph for each point in your answer. Here are a few ways to link your paragraphs together:

1) The beginning of a paragraph needs to show what the paragraph is about.

   One of the ways the poet presents the relationship in this poem is through her first person narrator.

   This makes it clear you're answering a question about how the poet presents the relationship in the poem.

2) You might want to link a new point with a previous paragraph.

   This is not the only way in which the poet develops the relationship in the poem.

   This refers back to the paragraph you've just finished.

3) You could show you're moving on to another topic.

   Form is also a very important part of this poem.

   This introduces your new topic.

4) You might be introducing a comparison or contrast within a poem.

   Although the narrator appears hurt by her lover's phone calls, she is still desperate to answer them.

   This word helps you start writing about a difference.

Use Different Words for the Same Thing

Make sure your paragraphs are full of interesting words. Don't fall into the trap of using the same word all the time — especially adjectives like "nice" or "weird".

The narrator of 'Sister Maude' is very angry. She's angry with her sister for telling their parents about her relationship. She sounds angry because of the angry language she uses.

It may be 'correctly' written, but it's not going to score you many points because it's so boring.

This is loads better. Using lots of different adjectives makes your answer more interesting.

The narrator of 'Sister Maude' is very angry. She is furious with her sister for telling their parents about her relationship. She sounds bitter because of the negative language she uses.

Pizza is nice, chocolate is nice, exams are NOT very nice...

Imagine how dull your essays will sound if you keep using the same old words all the time. Try to vary your sentences a bit so they sound more interesting. Your answer will sound loads better.

Glossary

adjective	A word that describes something, e.g. "big", "fast", "annoying".
alliteration	Where words that are close together start with the same letter. It's often used in poetry to give a nice pattern to a phrase. E.g. "hummed harmonics".
ambiguity	Where a word or phrase has two or more possible meanings.
assonance	When words share the same vowel sound but the consonants are different. E.g. "thumb / lung".
autobiographical	Describing something that happened in the poet's life.
ballad	A form of poetry that tells a story and often sounds quite musical.
blank verse	Poetry written in iambic pentameter that doesn't rhyme.
caesura	A pause in a line. E.g. Around the full stop in "I'm a hostage. I'm maroonded."
colloquial	Sounding like everyday spoken language, e.g. "the usual stuff".
consonance	When words have the same consonant sounds but different vowel sounds, e.g. "hurt", "heart".
consonants	All the letters in the alphabet that aren't vowels.
contrast	When two things are described in a way which emphasises how different they are. E.g. A poet might contrast two different places or two different people.
dialect	A variation of a language. People from different places might use different words or sentence constructions. E.g. The nonstandard grammar in "She runned away".
emotive	Something that makes you feel a particular emotion.
empathy	When someone feels like they understand what someone else is experiencing and how they feel about it.
end-stopping	Finishing a line of poetry with the end of a phrase or sentence.
enjambment	When a sentence runs over from one line or stanza to the next.
first person	When someone writes about themselves, or a group which includes them, using words like "I", "my" and "me".
form	The type of poem, e.g. a sonnet or a ballad and its features, like rhyme, rhythm, meter.
free verse	Poetry that doesn't rhyme and has no regular rhythm.
hyperbole	When a statement is exaggerated to make it stand out, e.g. "Vaster than empires".
iambic pentameter	Poetry with a metre of ten syllables — five of them stressed, and five unstressed. The stress falls on every second syllable, e.g. "My soul can reach when feeling out of sight".
iambic tetrameter	Like iambic pentameter but with a metre of eight syllables — four stressed and four unstressed. E.g. "She does the work about the house."
imagery	Language that creates a picture in your mind. It includes metaphors and similes.
internal rhyme	When a word in the middle of a line rhymes with the last word of the line. E.g. "Next time, you speak after the tone. I twirl the phone".
irony	When words are used in a sarcastic or comic way to imply the opposite of what they normally mean. It can also mean when there is a big difference between what people expect and what actually happens.
language	The choice of words used. Different kinds of language have different effects.

Glossary

Glossary

layout	The way a piece of poetry is visually presented to the reader, e.g. line length, whether the poem is broken up into different stanzas, whether lines create some kind of visual pattern.
metaphor	A way of describing something by saying that it is something else, to create a vivid image. E.g. "the parachute silk of his punctured lung".
metre	The arrangement of syllables to create rhythm in a line of poetry.
monologue	One person speaking for a long period of time.
mood	The feel or atmosphere of a poem, e.g. humorous, threatening, eerie.
narrative	Writing that tells a story, e.g. the poem 'Brothers'.
narrator	The voice speaking the words that you're reading. E.g. A poem could be written from the point of view of a young child, which means the young child is the poem's narrator.
oxymoron	A phrase which appears to contradict itself, because the words have meanings that don't seem to fit together, e.g. "comeliest corpse".
persona	A fictional character or identity adopted by a poet. Poets often create a persona so they can describe things from a different person's point of view, e.g. a male poet might use a female persona.
personification	A special kind of metaphor where you write about something as if it's a person with thoughts and feelings. E.g. "Love alters not with his brief hours and weeks".
rhyme scheme	A pattern of rhyming words in a poem, e.g. in 'Nettles', the 1st line rhymes with the 3rd, and the 2nd rhymes with the 4th.
rhyming couplet	A pair of rhyming lines that are next to each other, e.g. the last two lines of 'Hour'.
rhythm	A pattern of sounds created by the arrangement of stressed and unstressed syllables.
sibilance	Repetition of 's' and 'sh' sounds.
simile	A way of describing something by comparing it to something else, usually by using the words "like" or "as", e.g. "flying like a hare".
sonnet	A form of poem with fourteen lines, and usually following a clear rhyme pattern. There are different types of sonnets. They're often about love.
stanza	A group of lines in a poem. Stanzas can also be called verses.
structure	The order and arrangement of ideas and events in a piece of writing, e.g. how the poem begins, develops and ends.
syllable	A single unit of sound within a word. E.g. "All" has one syllable, "always" has two and "establishmentarianism" has nine.
symbolism	When an object stands for something else. E.g. A candle might be a symbol of hope, or a dying flower could symbolise the end of a relationship.
theme	An idea or topic that's important in a piece of writing. E.g. A poem could be based on the theme of friendship.
tone	The mood or feelings suggested by the way the narrator writes, e.g. confident, thoughtful.
voice	The personality narrating the poem. Poems are usually written either using the poet's voice, as if they're speaking to you directly, or the voice of a character.
vowels	The letters "a", "e", "i", "o" and "u".

Index

A
ageing 5, 39
aggressive language 7
ambiguity 13
anger 13, 15
animals 42, 50
Armitage, Simon 18, 32

B
ballads 13
Barrett Browning, Elizabeth 10
beginnings of poems 46
belief 21
betrayal 13
bitterness 23, 36
body 19
Born Yesterday 16, 34, 39, 46, 48, 52
Brothers 28, 35, 36, 41, 47, 49, 52, 68

C
caring 19
cherishing the moment 21
childhood 35, 37, 39
communication 25
comparisons 59
connectives (linking words) 69
constancy 5
controlled assessment 64
couplets 19, 47
cynical language 17

D
death 7, 40
desire 9, 43
devotion 5
dialect 9, 51
dramatic monologues 9, 13
Duffy, Carol Ann 20, 24

E
enjambment 25, 44, 45
example plans 56, 59, 62
example questions 65
exams 54
expectation 25

F
Farmer's Bride, The 8, 34, 36, 41, 42, 47, 48, 51, 53, 62, 63
fear 9
Fenton, James 22
first person narration 7, 19
food 31
Forster, Andrew 28
frustration 9, 29

G
getting older 39
Ghazal 26, 37, 42, 48, 50
gratitude 31
guilt 29

H
Harmonium 32, 40, 43, 51, 53, 63
helplessness 15
Hour 20, 37, 38, 49
humour 23, 33
hurt 25
hyperbole 7

I
imagery 50
impatience 7
In Paris With You 22, 35, 36, 43, 46, 49, 53, 66, 67
instructions 54

intense love 27
internal rhyme 23
irony 52

J
jealousy 13, 36
joy 31

K
Khalvati, Mimi 26

L
Larkin, Philip 16
last lines 47
love 11, 20, 21, 27, 37
lust 23

M
making comparisons 68
Manhunt, The 18, 34, 37, 41, 49, 55, 57, 66, 67
mark scheme 58
Marvell, Andrew 6
maturity 29
memory 41
Mew, Charlotte 8
military language 15
money and wealth 21
mood 53

N
narrative poems 15, 29
nature 9, 27, 42
negative emotions 36
Nettles 14, 34, 39, 41, 42, 46, 50, 52, 57, 68
Nichols, Grace 30

Index

O
ordinary language 17, 33

P
pain 15, 19, 43
paragraphs 71
Paris 23
patience 19
pleasure 21, 27
planning 56, 59, 62
playfulness 27
praise 31
Praise Song For My Mother 30, 37, 38, 42, 47, 50, 51, 66, 67

Q
Quickdraw 24, 35, 43, 51, 59, 60
quoting 70

R
regret 29
relationships 34, 35
religious language 11, 13
reluctance 7
repetition 11
revenge 15
rhyme 48
rhythm 48
rhyming couplets 5, 7, 17
Rossetti, Christina 12

S
sadness 33
sailing 5
sample answers 57, 60, 63
sample questions 55, 59, 62
sarcasm 52
Scannell, Vernon 14
self pity 23
Shakespeare, William 4
similarities and differences 68, 69
Sister Maude 12, 35, 36, 46, 48, 60, 66, 67, 71
Sonnet 43 10, 38, 40, 53
Sonnet 116 4, 39, 40, 47, 50
sonnets 5, 11, 44
speechlessness 33
spider diagrams 56

T
tables 56
tenderness 15
tension 25
three main ways to get marks 55, 65
time 5, 21, 33, 38
To His Coy Mistress 6, 34, 39, 40, 43, 52
true love 5

U
Unit 2: Poetry Across Time 54
Unit 5: Exploring Poetry 64
unselfish love 11
unusual vocabulary 51
urgency 7
use of first person 49

V
virtue 11

W
Westerns 25

Y
youth 29

Acknowledgements

The Publisher would like to thank:

For poems:
Simon Armitage: 'Harmonium' — Copyright © Simon Armitage
Simon Armitage: 'The Manhunt' — Reproduced with the permission of Pomona on behalf of Simon Armitage, 2008
Carol Ann Duffy: 'Hour' — From *Rapture* (Picador, 2005) reproduced with the permission of Picador, an imprint of Pan Macmillan, London. Copyright © Carol Ann Duffy 2005
Carol Ann Duffy: 'Quickdraw' — From *Rapture* (Picador, 2005) reproduced with the permission of Picador, an imprint of Pan Macmillan, London. Copyright © Carol Ann Duffy 2005
James Fenton: 'In Paris With You' — Reprinted by permission of United Agents on behalf of James Fenton
Andrew Forster: 'Brothers' — From *Fear of Thunder*, Flambard Press
Mimi Khalvati: 'Ghazal' — From *The Meanest Flower*, Carcanet Press Ltd (26 Jul 2007)
Philip Larkin: 'Born Yesterday' — From *The Less Deceived*, the Marvell Press, 1955, ISBN 978-0900533068
Grace Nichols: 'Praise Song For My Mother' — Reproduced with permission of Curtis Brown Group Ltd, London on behalf of Grace Nichols Copyright © Grace Nichols 1984
Vernon Scannell: 'Nettles' — From *New and Collected Poems* reproduced with the permission of Macmillan Children's Books, London, UK

For photographs:
Simon Armitage, Carol Ann Duffy, James Fenton, Grace Nichols — Rex Features
Elizabeth Barrett Browning, Andrew Marvell, Christina Rossetti, William Shakespeare — Mary Evans Picture Library
Andrew Forster — Andrew Forster/Flambard Press
Mimi Khalvati — Mimi Khalvati/Carcanet Press Ltd
Philip Larkin — Photograph by Godfrey Argent, Camera Press London
Charlotte Mew — Charlotte Mew/Carcanet Press Ltd

Every effort has been made to locate copyright holders and obtain permission to reproduce poems and images. For those poems and images where it has been difficult to trace the originator of the work, we would be grateful for information. If any copyright holder would like us to make an amendment to the acknowledgements, please notify us and we will gladly update the book at the next reprint. Thank you.